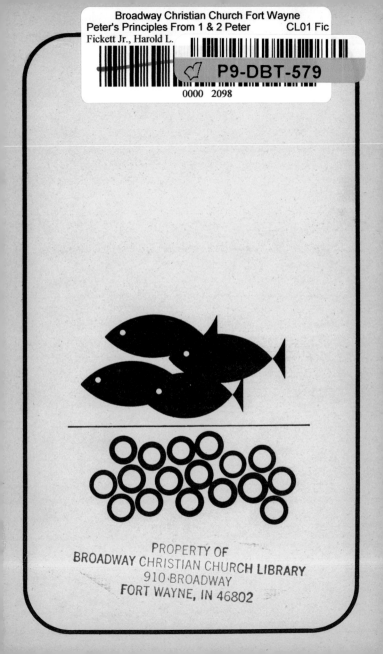

Peter's Principles

Harold L. Fickett, Jr.

A Division of G/L Publications
Glendale, California, U.S.A.

The basic Bible text used in this book is the *New American Standard Bible*.
© The Lockman Foundation, 1971. Used by permission. The following
symbols are used with Scripture verses quoted from other Bibles.

†Authorized Version (King James Version)

††*The Living Bible*, Paraphrased (Wheaton: Tyndale House, Publishers, 1971).
Used by permission.

Second Printing, 1974

Published by
Regal Books Division, G/L Publications
Glendale, California 91209, U.S.A.

Library of Congress Catalog Card No. 73-90620
ISBN 0-8307-0276-8

Contents

A teaching and discussion guide for individual or group study with this book is available in a G/L Teaching Kit from your church supplier.

Preface

From my pulpit at the First Baptist Church in Van Nuys I preached a series of fifty-three expository sermons on the books of 1 and 2 Peter. This volume is a distillation of that series. My prayer is that you will be spiritually benefited through reading it.

I would like to thank my two secretaries, Mrs. Eleanore Clodfelter and Mrs. Margaret Delbo, both for typing and proofreading the manuscript. Without their invaluable assistance I would have been hard pressed to complete the book.

May God bless you.

First Peter

1

---

1 Peter 1:1-9

SALUTATION

Generations ago a letter was written to a small group of Christians. It is probably the most beautiful, warm and flowing piece of literature to be found in the New Testament. That letter is the First Epistle of Peter.

As was the custom in those days, this letter began with a salutation: "Peter, an apostle of Jesus Christ, to those who reside as aliens, scattered throughout Pontus, Galatia, Cappadocia, Asia, and Bithynia." Four important words stand out clearly:

Peter

The name Peter indicates the human author of the book. It was he who was inspired by the Holy Spirit to write it. When he was born, his parents named him Simon. Our Lord Jesus Christ renamed him Peter or Cephas, the first being the Greek form, and the second the Aramaic. Both mean "a little rock."

What did Jesus mean when He said, "And I also say to you that you are Peter (Petros, 'a little rock'), and upon this rock (Petra, 'a big rock') I will build My church; and the gates of Hades shall not overpower it" (Matt. 16:17,18). "Peter" signifies "a little stone," while "Petra" (rock) means "a big immovable stone." The church is built on the latter—on Christ, the big, immovable "Rock."

Up until the nineteenth century, the fact was generally accepted that Simon Peter was the human author of the book. Toward the end of that century, however, the situation changed. Liberal scholars began casting doubts on the Petrine authorship. They argued (and continue to do so today) that Peter couldn't possibly have written it because he was only an uneducated fisherman. From the standpoint of rhetoric, the skilled use of the Greek language and smoothness of composition, it is the finest prose in the New Testament.

In Acts 4, where we are told that Peter and John defended themselves before the Sanhedrin for healing a crippled man, the members of the Sanhedrin "observed the confidence of Peter and John, and understood that they were uneducated and untrained men, (so) they were marveling" (v. 13). On the basis of this, some critics contend that Peter was a country bumpkin with no education whatsoever; he could not have composed such beautiful prose.

On the surface it looks as if they may be right. God anticipated this difficulty and neatly took care of it. "Through Silvanus, our faithful brother, . . . I have written to you briefly, exhorting and testifying that this is the true grace of God. Stand firm in it!" (1 Pet. 5:12). First Peter was written by Peter through Silvanus.

Who is Silvanus? Silvanus is the long form for Silas. Silvanus (Silas) traveled with Paul on his second missionary journey and is included with him in the salutation in First and Second Thessalonians. Silas was also one of the leading Christians of his day. (See Acts 15.)

Silas was with Paul on his second missionary journey when they were apprehended in Philippi and put into prison. God used them in a most unusual way in winning the jailer to Christ. In Acts 16 we find that Silvanus or Silas was a Roman citizen. As such he had the advantages of education and culture that were offered by Rome. Thus, he was far more educated than Peter. It was through him that the Big Fisherman (Peter), inspired by the Holy Spirit, produced the book of 1 Peter.

Simon Peter could have dictated the letter to Silvanus and then allowed him to correct it grammatically and to beautify its composition. Or he could have said in effect, "This is what I want in the letter," and let Silvanus write it in his own words.

Or perhaps Simon Peter made a rough draft of the letter and then gave it to Silvanus to edit. Regardless of how Peter did it, his use of Silvanus to compose this letter accounts for the Greek being excellent and the style beautiful.

Christians, driven from their homes and forced to live in alien places, must have welcomed Peter's letter with joy. It was written to help and comfort them during their trying times. Even though Peter used Silvanus to express his thoughts, it was Peter's love and concern that came through.

Apostle

An apostle is one sent from another person with credentials on a special mission. Peter, an apostle of Jesus Christ, was sent from the King of kings and Lord of lords, and was armed with power from God to perform miracles in His name. The story of Simon Peter and John going up into the Temple to pray shows how effective he was. As they approached the Gate Beautiful, a crippled beggar called out asking for money. Peter healed him instead. As a result, Peter had the opportunity of preaching to thousands of people that day, and five thousand men made decisions for Jesus Christ. Peter was a true apostle!

The privilege of being called an apostle belongs only to twelve specific men who were called and so named by the Lord Jesus Christ. After Judas Iscariot failed as an apostle, Simon Peter led the church to elect someone to take his place. But in God's own time He chose Paul to take the apostleship vacated by Judas Iscariot: "Paul, called as an apostle of Jesus Christ by the will of God" (1 Cor. 1:1).

While it is true there are only twelve apostles, it is likewise true that each Christian has been commissioned by the Lord Jesus Christ to be His ambassador. As such we have been spiritually armed with the credentials of love, truth, and compassion for others in order that we might, in the power of the Holy Spirit, effectively share the availability of redemption.

6

We who belong to Christ are to be apostles of love, compassion and concern for others.

Strangers

The third word in this first verse is "aliens." Dr. Kenneth Wuest describes the recipients of this letter as Christians who have "settled down alongside of" the unsaved. He then goes on to say, "Peter used this same word in (1 Peter) 2:11. He will not let us forget that we are living among the unsaved who are always carefully observing us."[1]

Nonbelievers are not concerned with what we say, only with what we do. Christians living alongside of nonbelievers are on display for them to see. Perhaps this is the reason many are turned off as far as Christ is concerned. They are not impressed with what they see in those who claim to love the Saviour.

Scattered

The word "scattered" tells why these early Christians were living in the provinces of Pontus, Galatia, Cappadocia, Asia and Bithynia. This word comes from the Greek *diaspora*. *Dia* means "through" and *spora* means "to sow or to scatter seed." From the Greek word *spora*, we get the word sperm which involves the idea of reproduction. The purpose of sperm is to reproduce, just as the main function of the Christian is to reproduce other Christians.

These first-century Christians were cast out of their homes by the Neronian persecution. They were literally scattered that they might sow the seed of the gospel which results in the reproduction of Christians.

Peter, after his salutation, talks about the triune

God and the three steps that He has taken to provide salvation for mankind. "According to the fore-knowledge of God the Father, by the sanctifying work of the Spirit, that you may obey Jesus Christ and be sprinkled with His blood: May grace and peace be yours in the fullest measure" (1 Pet. 1:2).

ELECTION

This first phrase clearly reveals the activity of God the Father. Here we are brought face to face with the doctrine of election. There are two philosophies as to its meaning. There are those who follow John Calvin and read the phrase, "Elect according to the foreknowledge of the Father" as if it read, "Elect according to the predestinating power of God the Father." These people insist that before the founda-tions of the earth, God elected some people to be saved and others to be lost. A man can do nothing to change this situation.

There are two biblical reasons why this philosophy of the doctrine of election cannot be true. We are made in the image of God and as such we are free moral agents who have the privilege on the basis of our will power to make choices that affect our destiny. (See Gen. 1:26,27.)

Adam had a choice which involved life or death, "And the Lord God commanded the man, saying, Of every tree of the garden thou mayest freely eat: but of the tree of the knowledge of good and evil, thou shalt not eat of it: for in the day that thou eatest thereof thou shalt surely die"† (Gen. 2:16,17). Adam made his choice of his own volition. God did not predetermine it for him.

8

The extreme Calvinist position of the doctrine of election is untenable because of what we know about the heart of God. His desire for all mankind is that everyone be saved. If God elected on the basis of His desire we would have universal redemption. Paul points this out eloquently, "This is good and acceptable in the sight of God our Saviour, who desires all men to be saved and to come to the knowledge of the truth" (1 Tim. 2:3,4).

There is a second philosophy propounded by many evangelists, including myself. We believe that Simon Peter meant exactly what he said. Bear in mind that there is a difference between foreknowledge and predestination. In the very heart of the greatest theological treatise that was ever written Paul points out this difference, "And we know that God causes all things to work together for good to those who love God, to those who are called according to His purpose. For whom He foreknew, He also predestined to become conformed to the image of His Son, that He might be the first-born among many brethren; and whom He predestined, these He also called; and whom He called, these He also justified; and whom He justified, these He also glorified" (Rom. 8:28-30).

The great missionary to the Gentiles says that God does not arbitrarily predestine some to go to heaven and others to go to hell. But God is omniscient. He knows how people will react in every situation. He created them as free moral agents and gives them the responsibility of making choices. It is on this basis that predestination is activated. Those whom He knows are going to accept Christ as Saviour, He predestinates to be conformed to the image of His Son.

Let me illustrate the difference between fore-knowledge and predestination. My wife and I have three grown children. While they were growing up, if a person had described for me a set of circumstances, I could have told him how each of our children would react to those circumstances. I could have done this not because I had predetermined the children's reactions, but because I knew them so well. And so it is with God. He has created all of us as free moral agents, but He knows how we are going to react in every situation.

The second step in the triune God's provision of salvation has to do with the ministry of the Holy Spirit. God the Father does the electing, but it is the Holy Spirit who brings the elected to the place of conviction and conversion.

The activity of Jesus Christ is the third step in the Trinity's provision of salvation. "And without shedding of blood there is no forgiveness" (Heb. 9:22). There has to be a blood atonement. Christ became that atonement by pouring His blood out on Calvary's tree. Those who by faith receive Him as Saviour and Lord become God's elect, sanctified by the Holy Spirit unto obedience to the faith.

GRACE AND PEACE

As Peter opens his letter with a prayer for the scattered Jewish people, his heart is filled with love for these believers. He implores Almighty God to bestow upon them a special measure of His grace and peace.

A careful scouting of the New Testament reveals that twenty of the twenty-seven books are letters. In fifteen of these twenty letters, including the thirteen that Paul wrote and the two that came from Peter's inspired pen, this prayer appears. The sequence of these two words "grace and peace" is always the same. This is an accurate and an important sequence not only in the Bible but also in life.

Today men are looking for peace in many places. They want a life-style that is satisfying, fulfilling, and that enables them to look to the future without fear. Some of our academicians are looking for this peace in philosophy and psychology. Both of these intellectual disciplines have their place. But separated from the grace of God, neither philosophy nor the application of psychology will result in peace.

Others vainly seek peace in the accumulation of wealth. There isn't much consolation in knowing that one day you will be the richest person in the cemetery. Others seek peace in psychedelic drugs, illicit sex and various religions, but it always escapes them. The Bible, God's written revelation to man, informs us that a life-style which is fulfilling and satisfying and enables us to look into the future without fear can only be had as we experience the grace of God.

The word "grace" comes from the Greek word *charis.* Kenneth Wuest wrote, "In the ethical terminology of the Greek schools *charis* implied ever a favor freely done, without claim or expectation of return."[2] Historically in evangelical circles "grace" has been defined as God bestowing unmerited favor upon a person. My favorite definition is, "Grace is God thinking in terms of what a man needs, rather than in terms of what he deserves."

God offers to man His grace on the level of salvation as the result of the death, burial and resurrection of the Saviour. Three classical passages in the New Testament spell this out for us. "For the grace of God has appeared, bringing salvation to all men" (Titus 2:11). All men are included in this offer. "But where sin increased, grace abounded all the more" (Rom. 5:20). No matter how abounding sin may be in your life, God's grace abounds more. "For by grace you have been saved through faith; and that not of yourselves, it is the gift of God; not as a result of works, that no one should boast" (Eph. 2:8,9). In grace He provides redemption; by faith we receive it. This results in our being at peace with our Creator. "Therefore having been justified by faith, we have peace with God through our Lord Jesus Christ" (Rom. 5:1).

And the best thing I know about this peace is that once we have it, we can never lose it. It is ours eternally. We can lose the joy of our salvation, our motivation for service and our rewards, but we can never lose peace with our Maker.

A friend of mine who was in the hospital recently said, "I have a cancerous blood disease. My doctor has informed me that I am confronted with three possibilities: (1) It may be a light case which medication will remedy; (2) It may be a case which can be controlled by medication but not cured; and (3) It could be fatal. If it is, my graduation exercises will occur sooner than I first thought." That man has peace with God.

The Almighty offers us day-by-day grace with which to meet the problems of life. This He does through the Holy Spirit who is in residence in our

12

lives. As He leads and we yield to that leadership, this problem-solving grace is poured out upon us. The necessary ingredient is willingness on our part to follow the Holy Spirit's directives.

I remember well September 2, 1946, the day Japan signed the surrender agreement, thereby ending World War II. Early that morning the ship which I served as chaplain took on board a Japanese pilot who directed us safely to our mooring place in Yokohama harbor. Had our skipper not been willing to listen to this pilot, we would have gotten into all kinds of difficulty. We arrived at our appointed place because we followed the directions of a man who knew where we were to go.

Like that pilot the Holy Spirit comes on board our lives when we receive Christ as Saviour. He takes up residence in our hearts; and as we yield to Him, He both leads us and gives us the grace to solve problems and overcome difficulties. This results in our having the peace of God in our lives, that warm, inward peace that enables us to know we are doing the will of God.

THE GREAT EULOGY

"Blessed be the God and Father of our Lord Jesus Christ, who according to His great mercy has caused us to be born again to a living hope through the resurrection of Jesus Christ from the dead, to obtain an inheritance which is imperishable and undefiled and will not fade away, reserved in heaven for you, who are protected by the power of God through faith for a salvation ready to be revealed in the last time" (1 Pet. 1:3-5).

Five basic Christian doctrines are suggested by these verses: (1) the fatherhood of God, (2) the new birth, (3) the resurrection of Christ, (4) the eternal inheritance of the Christian, and (5) the eternal security of the believer.

The Fatherhood of God

The word "blessed" is *eulogetos,* from *eulogeo.* We get our English word "eulogize" from this Greek verb. It is actually made up of two words, *eu* meaning "well" and *logeo* meaning "to speak." To eulogize a person means to speak well of him. Peter in the beginning of this verse says, "Eulogize or say something nice about the God and Father of our Lord Jesus Christ; the one who is the heavenly Father of all believers."

A little boy came home from Sunday School thrilled about his lesson. He said to his mother, "I learned something today I didn't know before. I learned what God's last name is, and it is not what Daddy said when he hit his thumb with a hammer." He then quoted, "God is love"; in so doing he was eulogizing the Almighty.

The New Birth

The next point has to do with the new birth. Peter calls attention to several facts concerning this great doctrine. It is God the Father who causes us to be born again. This is a true-to-life analogy for it is always the Father who does the begetting. It is not because we deserve it but because of His abundant mercy that He provides the new birth for us. The word "abundant" is intriguing; it is a translation of

14

the Greek *polu* which means "great" or "large." It is because of His large mercy, large enough to encompass the whole world, that a born-again experience is available to all people. The basic ideas in the concept of mercy include the existence of need and the ability and willingness on the part of someone to meet that need.[3]

In Jesus' story of the Good Samaritan (see Luke 10), the injured man had a need. The priest had the ability to meet it but not the willingness, so the act of mercy was not consummated. The same can be said of the Levite. But not so the Samaritan. He had both the ability and the willingness, so the act of mercy was completed. Each person has a tremendous need to become a part of God's eternal family through the new birth. By His Holy Spirit (1 Cor. 12:3) the Almighty has both the ability and willingness to meet that need.

The Resurrection of Christ

The next point flows out of the new birth for us and has to do with the resurrection of the Christian. The expression that Peter uses in verse 3 to describe it is a rather strange one but very meaningful. Implicit is the fact that the living hope of the Christian is the assurance of his ultimate victory over death based upon our Lord's resurrection.

The Big Fisherman wrote at a time when there seemed to be little if any hope in the world. "The gift of this living hope can be appreciated only by those who know the bondage of fear which held the pagan masses of that day captive. Those who were economically and politically well situated were surfeited with the fed-up life of luxury, or unsatisfied with the aimless and bankrupt pursuit of meaningless philosophical speculation. They knew nothing of real hope or joy or peace. While Greco-Roman civilization abounded with beauty, with courage, and with intellectual vigor, it was indeed a world without hope. Old age was faced with fear; life was continually threatened with misfortune and tragedy; and early death was to be desired above a life that at last had to end."[4] The philosopher Sophocles put it this way, "Not to be born at all—that is by far the best fortune; the second best is as soon as one is born with all speed to return thither whence one has come."[5]

The Christians had been driven out of their homes by persecution and were a part of the historical era characterized by abject hopelessness. It is quite significant to note that Peter writes about a living hope. There is a difference, you know, between a dead hope and a living one. I can say, "I hope that in tomorrow's mail I shall get a check for one million dollars from the most affluent man that ever lived." That is a dead hope. But on the other hand, I can say, "I hope that after finishing his second year in college my son will be coming home for the summer," and that is a living hope because it is according to the plan that our family has worked out. So it is with the living hope of the Christian. It is according to the plan devised by the omnipotent God of the universe.

The Eternal Inheritance

Peter then writes about the final inheritance of the Christian. The inheritance which God the Father guarantees the believer is incorruptible. This is a translation of the Greek *aphtharton* which literally means "free from corruption of any type." I have a trophy in my study that I won in a tennis tournament thirty-seven years ago. When I first received it, I thought it was pure gold. But such is not the case. It is now tarnished and rusty; it is worthless. Thank God, my eternal inheritance is not like this. It is free from corruption of any type.

Next, the Big Fisherman points out that the Christian's inheritance is "undefiled," a translation of the Greek *amianton*. This word is used to describe a mineral which was made into a fire-resistant cloth. Whenever this material got dirty the ancients cleansed it by putting it into a fire which would turn it pure white without destroying it. The Romans used it to wrap bodies of their deceased loved ones in preparation for cremation. The fire would penetrate it, burning the remains, but the cloth was not affected by the heat. It became the means by which the ashes were kept intact. And so it is with the believer's inheritance. It cannot be touched by the fires of judgment; it is an undefiled inheritance. Nothing can besmirch it or destroy it.

Following this Peter says that the believer's inheritance is "unfading." The Greek word which he uses here, *amaranton*, signifies that its beauty and loveliness is not affected by the passing of time. The Christian's inheritance does not wither and die. It is as eternal as God Himself is eternal. After describing our inheritance as believers as incorruptible, undefiled, and unfading, Peter goes on to say that it is reserved in heaven for us. The word used comes from *tereo* which means "to reserve," "to guard" and "to protect."

17

The Eternal Security

Peter teaches that not only is the inheritance of the Christian safe for time and eternity, but so is the believer himself eternally secure. The word translated "kept" in verse 5 is the Greek participle *phrouroumenous* which is a military term meaning "to be garrisoned about for the purpose of guarding and protecting." It is in the perfect tense which signifies that once an action has begun it will continue. The Big Fisherman actually tells us that while God is watching over our inheritance in heaven, we are being garrisoned about by His protective care, and this will continue until our salvation shall be consummated in glory.

The salvation God provides us in Christ Jesus is really in three parts:

1. Justification—the moment we accept Jesus Christ as Saviour and Lord, that moment we stand justified before God's eternal judgment bar.

2. Sanctification—after accepting Christ as our Saviour, the Holy Spirit takes up residence in our lives. As we yield to His leadership, He cleanses us and sets us apart (sanctifies) to be effective servants for the Saviour.

3. Glorification—when the Lord calls us to be with Him in eternity, either through death or the rapture, we are glorified in His presence.

PERIOD OF TESTING

God has not made and will not make the Christian way of life easy. He allows a believer's faith to be tested. Six truths are revealed concerning this testing process.

The time of the Christian's testing is short; he doesn't have to endure it forever. This is indicated by the phrase "though now for a season." *Oligon* is the Greek word translated "season." It literally means "little, small, few." Even though the period of testing may seem forever when the Christian experiences it—even though it may last for a lifetime—compared to eternity it is no longer than the snap of your fingers or the wink of your eye. How graphically the Psalmist spells this out, "Weeping may last for the night, but a shout of joy comes in the morning" (Ps. 30:5).

The phrase, "if need be" or "if necessary," implies that there is not always a need for a testing period. In the lives of some Christians the need seems greater than in others. As we look back into history we discover that the most prolific producers for the Saviour are those who faced the severest trials. A case in point is that of Paul (2 Cor. 11:24-28).

Sometimes the testings come as the result of Satan acting upon the lust of man, a thing God permits but never directs. This is implied by the word "temptations" which comes from the Greek *peirasmois* actually meaning "a temptation to do evil." James 1:13-15 spells out the fact that never is a Christian put to the test by God's directive will. He states bluntly in verse 13 that "God cannot be tempted by evil, and He Himself does not tempt any one." But this is not the way of Satan who is a past master at appealing to the lust that is inherent within man. Through this appeal he is often successful in persuading man to disregard the moral and ethical directives of Scripture and go on his own way. Every Christian needs to commit both to memory and to practice, "But remember this—the wrong desires that come into your life aren't anything new and different. Many others have faced exactly the same problems before you. And no temptation is irresistible. You can trust God to keep the temptation from becoming so strong that you can't stand up against it, for he has promised this and will do what he says. He will show you how to escape temptation's power so that you can bear up patiently against it"†† (1 Cor. 10:13).

The testings are of various types. They are described as being "manifold" which is a translation of *poikilois* which can also be translated "varied," "various," or "many colored." The word "heaviness" actually means "pain," "distress," "grief," or "sorrow." Peter is saying, "You are in grief and sorrow because of the many-colored testings confronting you."

In making this statement he had a specific situation in mind. It dated back to July 19, A.D. 64, the day Rome began to burn. This conflagration continued for three days and three nights. The culprit responsible for this was none other than Nero himself. As he watched the blaze from the Tower of Maecenas, he confessed that he was charmed with the flower and loveliness of the flame. All of the ancient landmarks were burned to the ground. Horrified at this, the people began to fix the blame on Nero. Naturally he had to find a scapegoat other than himself upon which the populace could vent their wrath. The only likely candidates for this were the Christians. He immediately began to persecute them, claiming that they were the perpetrators of the holocaust.

The historian Tacitus wrote concerning this spectacle, "Mockery of every sort was added to their deaths. Covered by the skins of beasts they were torn by dogs and perished, or were nailed to crosses, or were doomed to the flames and burned, to serve as a nightly illumination, when daylight had expired. Nero offered his gardens for the spectacle, and was exhibiting a show in the circus, which he mingled with the people in the dress of a charioteer, or stood aloft on a car. Hence even for criminals who deserved extreme and exemplary punishment, there arose a feeling of compassion; for it was not as it seemed for the public good but to glut one man's cruelty that they were being destroyed."[6]

In order to escape this savage death, many of the believers fled from their homes, seeking refuge in other parts of the world. Peter addressed this epistle to these refugee Christians.

Today the testings through which Christians go by the permissive will of God are many and varied. Sometimes they come in the form of financial reverses. Sometimes they come in the form of economic prosperity; some Christians find this very difficult to take for they have a tendency when all is going well to relegate God into a secondary place. Testing also appears in the form of sickness, accidents, domestic difficulties, tragedies of one type or another, and loneliness.

PURPOSE OF TESTING

The purpose of testings is purifying and proving: "That the proof of your faith, being more precious than gold which is perishable, even though tested by fire" (1 Pet. 1:7). Picture an ancient goldsmith who puts his gold ore into a crucible, subjecting it to intense heat. When the impurities rise to the surface, he skims them off. As soon as he can see his face clearly reflected in the liquid, he removes it from the fire for he knows he has pure gold. God as the eternal Goldsmith allows the Christian to undergo fiery trials in order that such impurities as obstinacy, willfulness, lack of faith, lack of concern, lack of compassion, and self-centeredness might be burned out of his life that he might become pure, reflecting in his very bearing the person of our Lord Jesus Christ.

The purpose of testing is to "prove" the Christian. The word "trial" should be translated "proving." It comes from the Greek *dokimazo* and it literally means "to put someone to the test with the expectation of showing that he is worthy of being approved." It was used in New Testament days to describe the final examination all medical students passed before they were given the right to set up their own practices. By going through trials in the power of the Holy Spirit, the Christian shows himself before God as a servant of Jesus Christ.

Peter points out the result for the believer who passes the tests which the Lord allows to come into his life: "May be found to result in praise and glory and honor at the revelation of Jesus Christ" (v. 7). *The Living Bible* translates this: "It will bring you much praise and glory and honor on the day of his return." As the faithful believer stands before the Judgment Seat of Christ He will hear the Master say, "Well done, good and faithful slave; you were faithful with a few things, I will put you in charge of many

22

things, enter into the joy of your master" (Matt. 25:21). There can be no greater reward than this!

LOVED THOUGH NOT SEEN

The Christians to whom Peter was writing were people who had never seen Jesus Christ with their physical eyes. He emphasizes this twice, "And though you have not seen Him, you love Him, and though you do not see Him now, but believe in Him, you greatly rejoice with joy inexpressible and full of glory" (1 Pet. 1:8). Although they had never seen Jesus Christ, they loved Him. Sometimes I talk with people who are convinced that if they could just see Jesus Christ with their eyes it would be very easy for them to follow Him and to be His disciples.

The public ministry of the Lord Jesus Christ is proof positive that this is not the case. Thousands of people directly benefited from what He taught, what He had to say, and by the miracles He performed. On one occasion He fed five thousand men with their wives and children, using only five loaves and two little fish. The Bible tells us that after they had all eaten, there were twelve baskets left over. And yet at the end of His ministry very few of these people thought enough of Him to be involved in His service. And so it was with the vast majority of people to whom the Saviour ministered. Even though they saw Him and were helped by Him, they did not love Him.

There is no real advantage in seeing Christ with the natural eye. The important thing is to see Christ through the eyes of faith. This is the experience of these people to whom Simon Peter wrote. They hadn't seen Jesus Christ as Simon Peter had; they hadn't heard Jesus Christ preach; they had never witnessed a miracle that He performed. The only picture they had of Jesus Christ is the picture that is given in the Old Testament and the picture that the apostles painted with their preaching. But as they looked at this picture through the eyes of faith they saw Jesus Christ as the Son of God, the Saviour of the world, and the Lord of life. And as they saw Him in this way they loved Him, believed in Him, and were ecstatic with joy.

Those of us living today have an advantage over the first-century Christians. We have the privilege of seeing Christ as He is presented in the Old Testament and also as He is portrayed in the New Testament. And as we look at Him from this vantage point we see Him loving us so much that He sacrificed Himself on Calvary and then conquered death that He might provide eternal redemption for us. We also see Him with His arms outstretched saying, "Come to Me, all who are weary and heavy laden, and I will give you rest" (Matt. 11:28).

Those of us who have seen Jesus Christ through the eyes of faith and have invited Him to be our Saviour and Lord have two special privileges. We are the object of His high priestly prayer in John 17. This was the prayer that fell from His lips just before He was betrayed by Judas Iscariot. "I do not ask in behalf of these alone, but for those also who believe in Me through their word" (v. 20).

And then He has a special blessing for us, "Blessed are they who did not see, and yet believed" (John 20:29). The word "blessed" comes from *makarios* which means "happiness to be envied." Let me para-

24

phrase the last part of this verse, "those who see Me through the eyes of faith find happiness which is to be envied."

Consistent in Love

These Christians who had been exiled were consistent in their love for Jesus Christ. We find this in the statement, "You love." The word for love is *agapate*. It is in the present tense which pictures continuous action. Peter is saying, "Even though you are in bondage, even though you are exiled and persecuted, even though you have never seen Jesus Christ, you love Him now and you are continuing to love Him. You just keep on keeping on loving Him."

The number one need in our churches today is the need for consistent love on the part of the Christians for Jesus Christ, a love that constantly expresses itself in giving. Someone has said that you can give without loving, but you can't love without giving. These people truly loved Jesus with a never-ending love, and Peter commended them for it. That is what God wants of each and every one of us.

Rejoicing Through Faith

Those exiled Christians were rejoicing Christians. They were happy Christians; they were Christians who were bubbling over because of their relationship with the King of kings and Lord of lords. And Peter infers that this happiness which they had was not derived from outward circumstances, but from their inward faith.

These Christians had come to know Jesus Christ

on the basis of a profound faith relationship. Even though their lives were difficult, they knew by faith that He would take care of their needs and enable them to solve their problems. Their happiness was derived from their relationship with Jesus Christ.

Let me ask, do you have a tendency to be unhappy? Do you have a tendency to sit in judgment on other people, or to be critical of them? Do you have a tendency to be miserable yourself and to make those around you miserable?

If you claim to be a Christian and your answer is yes, you had better examine yourself, for there are two possible reasons for this. You may be outside of God's will because of some unconfessed sin in your life. If this is the situation, I can assure you that you will not have any happiness until you take care of this problem. "If we confess our sins, He is faithful and righteous to forgive us our sins and to cleanse us from all unrighteousness" (1 John 1:9).

You may think you are a Christian when truthfully you are not. There are many in this category. They have professed Christ. They have been baptized, joined the church, taught Sunday School, been regular contributors to the work of the Lord, and they think they are Christians. While all of these things have their importance, they do not make an individual a child of God. This comes only by personally capitulating to Jesus Christ as his Saviour and Lord. If you have not done this, you are not a Christian and therefore the happiness which you desire has escaped you. You can have that desired happiness by surrendering yourself to the Lord.

The norm for the Christian is to be radiant, to

26

be bubbling over, to be excited about his faith, and to have an insatiable desire to share it with others. This is the way those exiled Christians were. This is the way God wants you and me to be.

Simon Peter calls attention to the fact that the final issue of faith is the salvation of the soul: "Obtaining as the outcome of your faith the salvation of your souls" (v. 9). In the Greek, the word for soul is *psuche*. It was used during the New Testament times in almost the same way as psychologists use the word "personality" today. It actually means "the person" or "the individual in the inner resources of his being." Simon Peter is telling us that the individual who sees Christ through the eyes of faith as Saviour and Lord and accepts Him as such, receives for himself the salvation of his person.

Footnotes

1. Kenneth Wuest, *First Peter in the Greek New Testament* (Grand Rapids: Wm. B. Eerdmans Publishing Co., 1942), p. 14.
2. Kenneth Wuest, *Treasures from the Greek New Testament* (Grand Rapids: Wm. B. Eerdmans Publishing Co., 1943), p. 16.
3. W. E. Vine, *Expository Dictionary of New Testament Words* (Westwood: Revell, 1940).
4. George Arthur Buttrick, ed., *The Interpreter's Bible,* Vol. XII (New York: Abingdon Press, 1957), p. 93.
5. William Barclay, *The Letters of James and Peter,* 2nd ed. (Edinburgh: The Saint Andrew Press, 1960), p. 169. See also *Tyndale Bible Commentary,* p. 203.
6. Barclay, *The Letters of James and Peter,* p. 177.

2

1 Peter 1:10-16

THE HOLY SPIRIT

Before we continue our study of First Peter, let me comment on different translations of the Bible. From time to time people come to me and say, "Pastor, don't you think the King James translation of the Bible is good enough? Why do we need so many modern translations?"

Translators in the year 1611, when the beautiful King James translation was brought into being, did not pay as much attention to details as translators today. As we look at verse 11 we discover that the King James translators made three mistakes. They refer to the Holy Spirit as "which," and they refer to Him as "it." Both "which" and "it" imply that the Holy Spirit is not a person but an influence. This agrees with the doctrine of Jehovah's Witnesses but is absolutely antithetical to the teaching of the Scripture. All the attributes of personality ascribed to the Lord Jesus Christ in the New Testament are also

31

ascribed to the Third Person of the Trinity. The third mistake is that the King James translators wrote the Greek *doxas* as "glory." It is in the plural and should be translated "glories." "And the glories that should follow" (v. 11).

DOCTRINE OF SALVATION

Peter wanted everyone who read his book to comprehend fully that which is involved in being saved. He wrote about the doctrine of salvation for he wanted to make the plan of salvation plain and clear for all of his readers. He calls to our attention three important facts: the means by which the prophets received the message of salvation; the secret of effective witnessing and the preaching of the doctrine of salvation; and the message of salvation which was proclaimed by the Old Testament prophets and preached by the New Testament apostles.

The Inspiration of the Message

The prophets received the message of salvation from the Spirit of Christ within them. This is just another way of saying that their message was inspired by the Holy Spirit. When they inquired as to the time this message applied, it was He who informed them that it was not for their generation but for those who lived following the death, the burial, and the resurrection of Jesus Christ.

The Secret of Witnessing

The secret of the effective witnessing and preaching of those early Christians in the New Testament days was the fact that they were filled with the Holy Spirit.

32

"It was revealed to them that they were not serving themselves but you in these things which now have been announced to you through those who preached the gospel to you by the Holy Spirit sent from heaven,—things into which angels long to look" (1 Pet. 1:12). That word "by" in the Greek is the little word "en." It means "in the power of the Holy Spirit." You and I, my friends, can be as eloquent as Demosthenes, poetic as Lord Byron, logical as Plato, and articulate as Apollos. But if we are not filled with the Holy Spirit in witnessing to others concerning our faith, our words are nothing more than "a sounding brass" or "a tinkling cymbal," and we might as well forget them. "And do not get drunk with wine, for that is dissipation, but be filled with the Spirit" (Eph. 5:18). Any Christian who prays to be filled with the Spirit will be. When he gives his testimony, he will not be giving it himself. It will be the Spirit of God and, consequently, it will be effective.

The Message of Salvation

The message of salvation which the Old Testament prophets proclaimed and the New Testament preachers preached is "seeking to know what person or time the Spirit of Christ within them was indicating as He predicted the sufferings of Christ and the glories to follow" (v. 11). The doctrine of salvation is consistently presented throughout both the Old and the New Testaments based on the sufferings of Christ and the glories that should follow.

One thousand years before the coming of Christ, David described the Crucifixion. "My God, my God, why hast Thou forsaken me?" (Ps. 22:1). These are

33

the exact words that our Lord uttered from the cross. "For dogs have surrounded me; a band of evildoers has encompassed me" (Ps. 22:16). As Christ was being crucified, His enemies gathered around the cross and hurled blasphemous remarks at Him. One of them said, "If you be the Christ save yourself and come down from the cross." Another suggested that if He were to do that, they would accept Him as the Son of God. Like dogs that were biting at His heels they were constantly at Him while He was hanging suspended between heaven and earth, pouring Himself as a blood sacrifice for you and for me. "They pierced my hands and my feet" (Ps. 22:16). That is what they did on Calvary. "I can count all my bones. They look, they stare at me; they divide my garments among them, and for my clothing they cast lots" (Ps. 22:17,18). You will recall, that the soldiers who were responsible for actually carrying out the order of execution shot dice for the robe of the Lord Jesus Christ.

Not only did the Old Testament prophets talk about the sufferings of Christ, they also talked about His resurrection. Once again David writes, "I have set the Lord continually before me; because He is at my right hand, I will not be shaken. Therefore my heart is glad, and my glory rejoices; my flesh also will dwell securely. For Thou wilt not abandon my soul to Sheol." There we have implied the Resurrection. "Neither wilt Thou allow Thy Holy One to see the pit." Once again we have the picture of the Resurrection. "Thou wilt make known to me the path of life; in Thy presence is fulness of joy; in Thy right hand there are pleasures forever" (Ps. 16:8-11). You and I don't have to guess as to the meaning of the passage, for Simon Peter in his pentecostal sermon quotes these verses from the Sixteenth Psalm and interprets them for us: "Brethren, I may confidently say to you regarding the patriarch David that he both died and was buried, and his tomb is with us to this day. And so, because he was a prophet, and knew that God had sworn to him with an oath to seat one of his descendants upon his throne, he looked ahead and spoke of the resurrection of the Christ" (Acts 2:29-31).

As we turn to the New Testament, we discover that there are many passages dealing with the sufferings and the glories of Jesus Christ. The apostle Paul has summarized them very well in his statement, "Have this attitude in yourselves which was also in Christ Jesus, who, although He existed in the form of God, did not regard equality with God a thing to be grasped, but emptied Himself, taking the form of a bond servant, and being made in the likeness of men. And being found in appearance as a man, He humbled Himself by becoming obedient to the point of death, even death on a cross" (Phil. 2:5-8). This describes the sufferings of Christ.

Paul goes on in the passage, "Therefore also God highly exalted Him, and bestowed on Him the name which is above every name, that at the name of Jesus every knee should bow, of those who are in heaven, and on earth, and under the earth, and that every tongue should confess that Jesus Christ is Lord, to the glory of God the Father" (vv. 9-11). Obviously this is a summary statement of the glories of the Saviour.

BE LIKE THE HOLY ONE

Yes, eternal transforming, redemption, based on the sufferings and glories of the Saviour, is available to all. And that word "all" includes you. "Therefore, gird your minds for action, keep sober in spirit, fix your hope completely on the grace to be brought to you at the revelation of Jesus Christ. As obedient children, do not be conformed to the former lusts which were yours in your ignorance, but like the Holy One who called you, be holy yourselves also in all your behavior; because it is written, 'You shall be holy, for I am holy' " (1 Pet. 1:13-16).

Peter begins this section with "therefore." In doing so it is as if he is saying, "Because God has done this for us, God expects certain things from us." Then he outlines some of these things in the words that immediately follow.

Before getting into the details of the text let us examine the last two verses. In these there is an unfortunate translation. As you and I read it there is a tendency on our part to say, "This is impossible. How can I possibly be as holy as the Lord Jesus Christ? He is perfect, and I am imperfect and finite. I cannot achieve this goal." The word "holy" is the Greek word *hagios*. It is also translated "saint," "saintly," "one that is worthy of admiration," "one that is worthy of honor," "one that is worthy of praise." You and I cannot possibly be worthy of praise and honor. We are far from saintly; we cannot possibly be as holy as our Lord Jesus Christ. But Peter does not use the word "be;" he has more intelligence than that. And the Spirit of God that inspired him to write was more intelligent than this. Instead of "be" he uses the word "become." "But like the Holy One who called you, become holy yourselves also in all your behavior; because it is written, 'You shall become holy, for I am holy'" (1 Pet. 1:15,16). It is a matter of becoming, not being; it is a process, not a fait accompli. We as Christians are to set Christ up a our example and we are to seek to become holy as He is holy. We will never make it; but, nevertheless, this should be our goal.

How are we going to do that? There are four demands in verses 13 and 14 that we must implement daily in our lives. Be mentally alert; be sober; be assured of our future; and be on the outside exactly what you are on the inside.

Be Mentally Alert

The first command has to do with the way in which the Christian uses his mind. He is to be alert mentally in learning what Christianity is all about. "Gird your minds" (v. 13). The Greek word for gird is *anazonnumi*. It calls to our minds a patriarch of the Old Testament who wore a long flowing robe. Around that robe he had a big belt called a girdle. When the time came that he had to move swiftly, he pulled it up and lapped it over the belt. He girded up his loins and was ready for action.

In giving this command, Peter was saying, "Now that you've become a Christian, roll up your sleeves, take off your coat, and move quickly to learn what Christianity is all about. Study the great doctrines of the faith so that you will not be spiritually illiterate."

We have a man who found Christ in our church

37

about six months ago. After he received Jesus Christ as his Saviour, he felt the need of learning what Christianity was all about, and so he rolled up his sleeves and went to work. He is studying the Word of God from one to three hours every day. So intrigued is he by what the Bible says that he has gone to the bookstore and bought innumerable commentaries and has read them and studied them very carefully. He is growing rapidly into a mature Christian. He is a busy, successful, affluent man. He spends twelve hours in his office many, many days, and yet takes time to make sure that he is not a spiritual illiterate.

Paul emphasizes this truth, "I urge you therefore, brethren, by the mercies of God, to present your bodies a living and holy sacrifice, acceptable to God, which is your spiritual service of worship. And do not be conformed to this world, but be transformed by the renewing of your mind" (Rom. 12:1,2). That word "renew" is the Greek verb *anakainoo*. It means "to cause to grow," or "to cause to mature." What Paul is saying is this, "Every Christian needs to mature mentally in the faith; this will result in his perceiving a complete transformation of life."

The main problem we have in Christianity is that most people who have their names on church rolls are simply emotional Christians. They have been moved emotionally to accept Jesus Christ as Saviour and Lord, and that's wonderful. I would not deprecate that experience. I'm all for emotion. But it is equally important that we don't let our Christianity stop there.

Every Christian should read the entire Bible every year, thereby becoming knowledgeable as to what

God's Word is all about. This enables him to be spiritually literate and not just an emotional believer.

Be Sober

The second command centers around the theme of sobriety. Peter writes, "Keep sober." This is a translation of *nephontes* which literally means, "Don't get drunk." Metaphorically it means that the Christian is to live a self-disciplined, spirit-controlled life on the basis of the ethical and moral teachings of God's Word. He is like an athlete who, because he wants to win, regulates his life on the basis of the training rules spelled out by his coach. .

Be Assured of Our Future

Peter tells us we are to be assured of our future. "Fix your hope completely on the grace to be brought to you at the revelation of Jesus Christ" (v. 13). This latter phrase, "the revelation of Jesus Christ," is a reference to the coming of Christ for His Church. In theological jargon it is called the rapture of the Church. The grace that will be brought to those of us who are Christians at that time is our complete glorification. You and I have mortal bodies which are subject to corruption and death. When the Lord returns, those of us who are a part of His Church are going to receive our glorified bodies. It doesn't make any difference whether we are dead or alive. We are going to experience victory over all the forces of evil; even death itself.

There are some other matters in this command that we need to look at. The word "hope" as it is used in the New Testament is not the way you and I use it today. When I say, "I hope I am going to get this," I really mean, "I wish that I could get this." But the word "hope" in the New Testament is much stronger than this. W. E. Vine in his *Expository Dictionary of New Testament Words* tells us that it means "favorable and confident expectation." The word "hope" is a verb, and in the Greek here, it is in the aorist tense, meaning a once-and-for-all action. Once and for all we are to put our hope in the future that God has in store for us. The final phrase of the command is a poor translation of the Greek word *teleios* which really means "completely and perfectly." We are told that our glorification is to be brought to us. A more accurate translation would be, "It is on its way." Now let me paraphrase the command so that we can see what is actually involved in it. "Have complete and perfect confidence in the fact that your full glorification is on its way and will be finally realized when Christ comes for His Church."

Kenneth Wuest points out that in the bill of fare that God serves mankind, there are three main courses: the first is justification. When an individual accepts Jesus Christ as Saviour and Lord, he becomes justified before the judgment bar of God. The second is sanctification. After a person has accepted Christ as Saviour and allows the Spirit of God to indwell him, taking control of his life, the Spirit sanctifies him. He cleanses him and sets him apart for the job that God wants him to do. Now these two courses have been and are being served right now. The third course that God serves is on its way. It is the course of glorification; the receiving of our incorruptible, immortal bodies. Kenneth Wuest puts it this way,

"It is like eating a bountiful repast at the home of Mrs. Charming Hostess. While we are enjoying the delicious meal, we are not worrying whether there will be dessert or not. We know it is on the menu, and is being brought to us as soon as we are ready for it."[1] God serves justification; that's wonderful! We stand before the judgment bar of God just as though we had never sinned. He serves us sanctification, if we will let Him; it equips us to do the job that God wants us to do. And the dessert is the best of all. The individual who has his faith firmly fixed in this can withstand almost anything.

Demonstrate Our Faith

The fourth command is an interesting one. We are not to conduct ourselves outwardly as we did before we became Christians. We have become new creations in Christ as the result of our faith in Him. Now by our works, outwardly, we are to demonstrate this. But Peter is not the only one who talks about this. Jesus speaks about it in the Sermon on the Mount. "You are the light of the world. A city set on a hill cannot be hidden" (Matt. 5:14).

James emphasizes this same truth in James 2:14-16. He says that if you claim that you are a Christian, if you claim that you have faith, and your works do not back up your faith, then you are not telling the truth; you are a liar.

Footnotes

1. Kenneth Wuest, *First Peter in the Greek New Testament* (Grand Rapids: Wm. B. Eerdmans Publishing Co., 1942), p. 36.

3

1 Peter 1:17-25

THE PERSON OF GOD

Many and varied are the word pictures of God given to us in the Old and New Testaments. The Big Fisherman portrays Him as a Father, a Judge, and a Redeemer: "And if you address as Father" (v. 17). This is a Greek construction which can be translated, "Since you call God your Father," or "Because you have the right to call God your Father." It is shocking for some people to learn that not every one has the right to call God his Father. There are imposters today who call God their Father. They do this because they subscribe to the erroneous idea that God is the universal father of man and therefore all men are brothers. God is the Creator of all, but not the Father of all.

As Father

Who has a right to call God Father? Those who have been born into the family of God through faith in Jesus Christ as Saviour and Lord. There is only one brotherhood which the Almighty recognizes and that brotherhood is in Christ Jesus. The Mohammedan has ninety-nine names for God, but Father is not one of them. When you and I accept Jesus Christ as Saviour we are born into the family of God, and from then on we know the omnipotent God of the universe as our own Father.

As we look into the Scripture we discover that Father God does a number of things for His Children. As our heavenly Father, God is willing to answer our prayers. Jesus spoke of this in the Sermon on the Mount. (See Matt. 7:7-11.)

He forgives our sins when we request Him to do so. I am so thankful for 1 John 1:9: "If we confess our sins, He is faithful and righteous to forgive us our sins and to cleanse us from all unrighteousness." God will cleanse sin; He will give us a bath on the inside. Our Father chastises us when we need it. "And you have forgotten the exhortation which is addressed to you as sons, 'My son, do not regard lightly the discipline of the Lord, nor faint when you are reproved by Him; for those whom the Lord loves He disciplines, and He scourges every son whom He receives'" (Heb. 12:5,6).

When He chastises us, He does so because we need it in order to get straightened out in our thinking and actions, and because He really loves us. Instead of resenting this chastisement, we should be grateful for it and profit by it.

The Word of God reveals that our heavenly Father not only answers our prayers, forgives our sins, and disciplines us, but He also meets our needs, especially those that are eternal. Jesus beautifully expressed this: "Let not your heart be troubled; believe in God, believe also in Me. In My Father's house are many dwelling places; if it were not so, I would have told you; for I go to prepare a place for you. And if I go and prepare a place for you, I will come again, and receive you to Myself; that where I am, there you may be also" (John 14:1-3).

Peter also presents God as Judge. "And if you address as Father the One who impartially judges according to each man's work, conduct yourselves in fear during the time of your stay upon earth; knowing that you were not redeemed with perishable things like silver or gold from your futile way of life inherited from your forefathers, but with precious blood, as of a lamb unblemished and spotless, the blood of Christ" (1 Pet. 1:17-19).

Before we actually get into our consideration of this second major emphasis, notice this command, "Conduct yourselves in fear during the time of your stay (here)." In order to understand what is involved in this command it is necessary that we understand Peter's meaning of the words "stay" and "fear."

The word "stay" comes from the Greek *paroikia* and means a temporary visit in a foreign land. A child of God is a visitor here on earth. He is a pilgrim. He has no permanent citizenship here.

The word "fear" comes from the Greek *phobos*. In verse 17 it means "reverence" or "respect." William Barclay helps us understand the meaning of this word: "Reverence is the attitude of mind of the man who is always aware that he is in the presence of God. It is the attitude of the man who speaks every word and performs every action and who lives every moment conscious of God."[1]

So Peter is saying, "During the short time that you are here on earth, make sure all that you do and say is motivated by your love and respect for Almighty God." We obey this command because God is our Judge. He is not only our Father, but He is our Judge.

As Judge

When Christians think about God as a judge, two judgments immediately come to mind. The judgment seat of Christ (2 Cor. 5:10), which every Christian faces, is not for the purpose of ascertaining whether or not we are saved. It is to determine how faithful we have been in serving Jesus Christ. On the basis of this determination we will be given our rewards.

The second judgment that comes to mind is the judgment of the great white throne (Rev. 20:11-15). Only those who have rejected Christ will appear at that judgment. They are there to be judged as to the degree of punishment they will suffer in hell.

Neither one of these judgments is in Peter's mind as he writes this passage we are studying. The judgment he has in mind is the judgment of every believer that God is carrying on right now. Did you know that if you are a Christian you are being judged every moment by God Himself as to how faithful you are in serving Christ? As to how involved you are in making your time, talent and treasure count for Christ? God is not impressed with how successful you are in life. You don't make Brownie points with Him simply because you accumulate a lot of money. You don't impress Him because you are the best doctor, dentist, lawyer or businessman in your community. That is all well and good if you use it to His glory. God expects you to be involved in serving Christ regardless of how successful you are. The word used for judging here is from *krino*, which means to judge that which is good. Let's combine this idea with God as the Father. God as the Father is constantly judging you and me as Christians because we are His children. The purpose of His judging us here and now is that He might find something for which He can commend us.

As Redeemer

Not only is God Father, not only is God Judge, but God is also Redeemer. And only as we know Him as our Redeemer can we know Him as Father.

The redemption God has provided for man results in his being delivered from an empty and vain life. The word "vain" is the Greek word *mataios* and it actually means "striving for something that is never achieved." People outside of Christ are constantly striving for happiness and satisfaction, but they never make it.

Regardless of how successful the non-Christian may be in the business and professional world, the life that he lives when measured in terms of eternity is vain and empty. No one knew this any better than some of these Jewish people who had been converted. They had received a religion by tradition from their fathers; and through that religion, they were trying to find a life-style that pleased them. They were trying to find satisfaction. They did everything they were supposed to do but their lives lacked fulfillment. Judaism was dead. The One who could have given life to it, Jesus Christ, had been rejected.

There are many Jewish people like this today. They are looking for a life-style that will meet their needs but they are not finding it. And there are many so-called Christians in the same boat. Their names are on church rolls, but they have never experienced Christ. Theirs is simply a traditional religion in which they have no vital relationship with the Saviour.

The redemption that God makes available to us has been purchased at a very high price. Peter states the price of our redemption both negatively and positively. Negatively he puts it this way: "Ye were not redeemed with corruptible things." This suggests the picture of a common scene in his day, a slave being purchased at auction. In effect Peter is saying, "Silver and gold are corruptible commodities and therefore cannot be used to purchase your redemption from the slave market of sin."

Positively Peter informs us that the price of our redemption is the precious blood of Jesus Christ who is a lamb without spot and without blemish. This takes us back into the Old Testament. God and Pharaoh were having a contest. The Almighty through Moses and Aaron was demanding that the Egyptian ruler let the children of Israel go free, and He backed up His demand with a series of plagues. The last plague was the death of the firstborn son in each Egyptian home. God told the people of Israel to select a lamb and on the night of Passover to slay the lamb and smear its blood around the front door. "And the blood shall be a sign for you on the houses where you live; and when I see the blood I will pass over you, and no plague will befall you to destroy you when I strike the land of Egypt" (Exod. 12:13). They were saved by the blood of that Passover lamb.

John the Baptist, in calling his disciples' attention to the Lord Jesus Christ, declared, "Behold, the Lamb of God who takes away the sin of the world!" (John 1:29). The price of your redemption and mine is His blood shed on Calvary. Peter describes it as "precious." In the Greek it is the word *timio* which means "costly" and "highly esteemed" or "held in honor." The price of our redemption was exceedingly costly to Almighty God because it involved the death of His Son. Is it any wonder that the true believer holds it in honor and highly esteems it?

The plan of redemption that God has provided for us predates history. "For He was foreknown before the foundation of the world, but has appeared in these last times for the sake of you" (v. 20). God's redemptive plan was no afterthought on His part. Long before the world was brought into being, long before you and I were created, the triune God set aside Jesus Christ to die on Calvary that we might have our sins forgiven.

Man's redemption is available through Jesus Christ whom God raised from the dead and gave a place of glory. If we accept Him as Saviour and Lord, we are not only putting our faith in Him, but through Him we are placing our faith in God the Father, and the Holy Spirit. We have a faith relationship with the triune God: "Who through Him are believers in God, who raised Him from the dead and gave Him glory, so that your faith and hope are in God"

(v. 21). And it makes no difference what your position in life is. The moment you accept God's offer of redemption by faith you have a never-ending personal relationship with the Father, Son, and Holy Spirit.

AN OBVIOUS CONTRAST

"Since you have in obedience to the truth purified your souls for a sincere love of the brethren, fervently love one another from the heart, for you have been born again not of seed which is perishable but imperishable, that is, through the living and abiding word of God. For, 'all flesh is like grass, and all its glory like the flower of grass. The grass withers, and the flower falls off, but the word of the Lord abides forever.' And this is the word which was preached to you" (1 Pet. 1:22-25).

The spiritual aspect of this passage actually flows upstream. Therefore, it is logical that we look at verses 24 and 25 first, then at verse 23 and finally at verse 22. As we begin our examination at verses 24 and 25 we discover that Peter is presenting an obvious contrast between man in his natural state, and the Lord Jesus Christ who is the living Word of God.

Each year when spring comes after a hard winter, nature brings about a resurrection. The grass turns green, the flowers bloom. But following summer comes autumn, and the first freeze. At that point the grass turns brown, and all of the flowers disappear. Peter said that this is the way man is. He has his days when he is "green" and his accomplishments are like the flowers, but that first freeze will inevitably come. And when it does, the grass turns brown in death, and the flowers symbolizing his accomplishments are forgotten even by those who are closest to him. This is Simon Peter's poetic way of pointing out that if the Lord delays His coming, every one of us is going to experience death.

In contrast to this, "the word of the Lord abides forever" (v. 25). It is the living Word of the Lord, even ˈesus Christ. Man dies, but the Lord Jesus Christ endures forever. Peter's message was centered in the living Word, Jesus Christ, man's only sufficient Saviour.

In verse 23 we learn that they accepted this message and a miracle happened. When Jesus Christ was preached to these people, they accepted Him as Saviour and Lord and as a result, they had a spiritual birth. They were born of incorruptible seed. This gave them the assurance that just as the living Word abides forever, they too possessed eternal life.

Peter commends them in verse 22 for loving their Christian brothers and he commands them to love their Christian brothers. Was Simon Peter confused? Why on the one hand would he commend them for loving, and on the other hand command them to love? The answer is to be found in the words that are translated "love." In his commendation he uses *phileo,* "friendship." These Christians had reached the "friendship plateau" in their interpersonal relationships. This was fine, but it was not enough. In the command, *agapao* is used which means to love as God loves. Paul uses this word when he writes, "But God demonstrates His own love toward us, in that while we were yet sinners, Christ died for us" (Rom. 5:8).

I read a story the other day that really illustrates

this type of godly love. It centers around a fourteen-year-old boy back in the days when blood transfusions consisted of pumping the blood out of one person's veins directly into those of the patient. This boy had a little crippled sister who was stricken with a malady that doctors said would eventuate in her death unless she had a blood transfusion. When he heard this, he immediately said, "I'll give her my blood." So this boy lay down on the table next to his sister, and the transfusion took place. Following this the boy was instructed to stay on the table and rest. In about thirty minutes when the doctor reentered the room the boy asked, "Doctor, when am I going to croak?" That boy actually believed that by giving his sister his blood, he was going to die. He loved her so much that he was willing to do this.

Footnotes

1. Barclay, *The Letters of James and Peter,* p. 222.

4

1 Peter 2:1-10

ELIMINATE THE NEGATIVE

The second chapter begins, "Because you have received all these blessings, you have to eliminate the negative and accentuate the positive in your life." In verse 1 Peter makes a list of five negatives. And in verses 2 and 3, he points out a daily spiritual exercise to accentuate the positive. Zero in on that first verse with me. "Therefore, putting aside. . . ." This portrays a man taking off his coat in order that he might make faster progress. There are certain negatives that we have to eliminate that they might not inhibit our progress in the Christian life: malice, all guile, hypocrisies, envies and all evil speakings.

Malice

Malice is a synonym for "wickedness." In Acts 8, it is used in the sense of "scheming to get ahead." Simon, the sorcerer, schemed to get the ability to put his hands on people that they might receive the Holy Ghost. He tried to buy it. When he made his offer Peter said, "Your silver perish with you" (Acts 8:20). Scheming to get ahead won't get the job done.

Guile

We are to eliminate all "guile," which basically means "deceit." It also is used in the New Testament in the sense of scheming for the purpose of destroying something or someone. We have an example of this in Matthew 26:3,4. There we find the writer talking about the enemies of Christ. They knew that they couldn't openly apprehend Him, bring Him to trial and kill Him. He was too popular with the people. So they began to scheme to destroy Him.

Hypocrisy

Peter tells us that we are to eliminate all destructive scheming and get rid of all hypocrisy. In Matthew 23:3 Jesus gives us the best definition of a hypocrite to be found anywhere in literature. He applies it to the religious leaders of that day. "They say, and do not." Who is a hypocrite? A hypocrite is one who says that he loves Christ, but he refuses to be involved in serving Him.

Would you like to see Christ's evaluation of a hypocrite? Look at Matthew 23:29,33. Here He plainly states that hypocrites are snakes and vipers. You talk about straightforward preaching, this is it! Hypocrisy does more to turn people away from Christ than almost anything I know.

Some people are afraid to accept Jesus Christ as Saviour until they are sure that they can live without hypocrisy. This is like driving an automobile without a motor. You cannot do it because of a lack of power. First comes faith, then the power of God's Spirit. As you yield to Him daily, He enables you to eliminate hypocrisy from your life.

Envy

Peter also tells us that we are to get rid of all envy which is the deadliest of sins. In Mark 15 we have the story of Jesus on trial before Pilate, who has a great desire to release Him. "For he was aware that the chief priests had delivered Him up because of envy" (Mark 15:10). Jesus had become the people's spiritual leader instead of the priests, and they couldn't take it. Humanly speaking, envy actually brought about the death of Jesus Christ. Envy destroys happiness; it destroys peace of mind; it destroys family relationships; it destroys relationship to God; and it can even motivate murder. The person who is victimized by this evil cancer is no good to himself, no good to his family and no good to the Lord. Is it any wonder that Peter admonishes us to get rid of all envy?

Evil Speaking

In the last negative point Peter declares we are able to eliminate "all evil speakings." Gossip, backbiting and slander are synonyms for evil speaking. The Bible says more against gossip than against murder, adultery, or any other sin. Gossiping is worse than hypocrisy, although usually the two go together.

Some of you will say, "I want to eliminate my

tendency to gossip and all of those other negatives. But how can I do it?"

In effect Simon Peter writes, "You have to eliminate these things, you know that. You are also aware that to resolve to do so is not enough. You have to accentuate the positive as newborn babes, as new Christians, by having an insatiable desire for the pure, unadulterated, nourishing milk of God's Word whereby you can grow spiritually. Set aside a time in which to fill yourself daily with the truths of God's Word. And this you will do if you have tasted and found that the Lord is gracious." (See 1 Pet. 2:2,3.)

Instead of scheming to get ahead, you'll rejoice when others get ahead. Instead of scheming to destroy some program that God is blessing, you'll pray for it. Instead of being a hypocrite, you'll sit in judgment of yourself. When you find that you have done wrong, you will put 1 John 1:9 into practice. Instead of being envious of others, you'll be thrilled when good things come into their lives. And instead of gossiping about people who are members of the body of Christ, you will pray for them.

THE LIVING STONE

The living Stone and the Rock are symbols of Christ used throughout Scripture. In the first place, the Saviour is spoken of as the Stone that was smitten or the Rock that was struck. This metaphor draws our attention to the Old Testament.

Twice during their wilderness wanderings the Israelites found themselves without water. The agonies of thirst caused them to turn against Moses instead of turning to God. Nevertheless, God provided for them by giving them water from a rock. The first time, Moses struck the rock under God's instructions. The second time, he was supposed to speak to the rock, but he struck it twice. Even so, God provided the water. (See Exodus 17 and Numbers 20.)

We don't have to guess what the symbolism of this rock is. The Bible makes it very clear: "And all drank the same spiritual drink, for they were drinking from a spiritual rock which followed them; and the rock was Christ" (1 Cor. 10:4). The Rock that was struck is symbolic of the Lord Jesus Christ in His crucifixion.

God did for the children of Israel what they couldn't do for themselves. They were about to die. If God had not provided water, they would have died. But God, because He loved His covenant people, provided water for them out of the rock. That water was free, and there was an abundance of it sufficient to meet all of their needs. This is what God has done for man through the Rock of Ages, the Lord Jesus Christ. He has provided redemption free for him. He has provided the Water of Life, free for everyone.

Foundation Stone

In the second place, Christ is presented as the Foundation Stone, or the Foundation Rock, of the Christian's life. "For no man can lay a foundation other than the one which is laid, which is Jesus Christ" (1 Cor. 3:11). He is the only one with structural strength sufficient to form a foundation in the life of every believer. (see Matt. 7:24-27.)

Chief Cornerstone

In the third place, Jesus Christ is pictured as the Chief Cornerstone of the church. In Matthew 21:33-43 Jesus tells of a very rich land owner who planted a vineyard and turned it over to some tenant farmers. When the time came for the owner to receive his share of the profits, the tenants killed a series of servants sent by the owner, and they finally killed the owner's son. (See Matt. 21:33-43.)

Jesus applied the parable thus: "Did you never read in the Scriptures, 'The stone which the builders rejected, this became the chief cornerstone; this came about from the Lord, and it is marvelous in our eyes'?" (v. 42). We understand immediately that the heir, the son that is involved, is none other than Jesus Christ. Paul picks up this idea and applies it to Christ and the church. He writes: "So then you are no longer strangers and aliens, but you are fellow-citizens with the saints, and are of God's household, having been built upon the foundation of the apostles and prophets, Christ Jesus Himself being the cornerstone, in whom the whole building, being fitted together is growing into a holy temple in the Lord" (Eph. 2:19-21).

Peter adds his "Amen" to Paul's teaching as he writes, "For this is contained in Scripture: 'Behold I lay in Zion a choice stone, a precious cornerstone, and he who believes in Him shall not be disappointed.' This precious value, then, is for you who believe, but for those who disbelieve, 'The stone which the builders rejected, this became the very cornerstone' " (1 Pet. 2:6,7). Almighty God has made the Lord Jesus Christ the Chief Cornerstone of the Church.

In the fifth verse, Simon Peter also points out that each and every one of us is a living stone if we love Jesus Christ. And as a living stone, we are to be built into the Church. The Spirit of God is constructing the Church. You and I that love Jesus Christ are the building stones for doing this. And Jesus Christ is the chief cornerstone.

In this connection William Barclay has written that the Christian is likened unto a living stone, and the Church is likened unto a living edifice into which he is built. Clearly, that means that Christianity is community. The individual Christian finds his true place only when he is built into the edifice of the Church. Solitary religion is ruled out. Barclay goes on to say, "So long as a brick lies by itself it is useless. It only becomes of use when it is built into a building. That is why it was made; and it is in being built into a building that it realizes its function and the reason for its existence. It is so with the individual Christian. To realize his destiny he must not remain alone, but must be built into the fabric and edifice of the Church."[1]

We as Christians need one another for we can't stand alone. Since this is true, we must recognize the fact that we can't have everything in the church according to our own desires. There are parts of the program that may not please us and may not do anything for us, but God uses them to reach others for the Lord Jesus Christ. Our realization of this will motivate us to pray for the total church program. And it will enable us to get out of the nit-picking business.

During a recent evangelistic campaign, the special

music each night was presented by an unusual trio who really sang with a beat. One of our men said, "When I heard that trio begin to sing, I started to get up and walk out. Then I thought that maybe the trio was doing something for others that it was not doing for me. I decided to just sit there and pray. How glad I am that I did. I have a nineteen-year-old boy. For two years I have been trying to get him to come to church, but he wasn't interested. When he heard about this trio, he came. Night after night he was there. During one of the services the Spirit of God spoke to him and he turned his life over completely to the Lord Jesus Christ. One night he and I were having a good talk and I asked him what caused him to make his decision for Christ. He answered, 'Don't you recall the words that were sung by that trio? They sang their message right into my mind and heart, and I could do nothing else but let Christ take control.' How glad I am that I didn't walk out on them.

Christianity is community!

Stone of Stumbling

In the fourth place, Jesus Christ is presented as the Stone of Stumbling and the Rock of Offense. (See 1 Pet. 2:8.) From the inception of Christianity, the Lord Jesus Christ was a stumbling stone and a rock of offense to His own people, the Jews. The reason for this was that they did not understand their own Scriptures, the Old Testament. They had conceived of the Messiah simply coming as King of kings and Lord of lords. They had overlooked that great section of Scripture in the Old Testament that talks

64

about the Messiah coming and dying for the sins of mankind. So, He became for them a stumbling stone and a rock of offense. For most of the Jews today, He is still the same. Because He did not set up His earthly kingdom at His first coming, they think of Him as a martyr who died for the cause he was espousing. They consider Him to be only a man. This is not the way it is always going to be. In Zechariah 12:10 we are told that when the Lord comes, the Jewish people, God's chosen, are going to look upon Him whom they have pierced and are going to mourn as one mourns for an only son.

For years Jesus Christ has also been a stone of stumbling and a rock of offense for many Gentiles. One day I talked to a man who knows the gospel as well as I do. When I asked why he didn't turn his life over to Christ, he said, "Listen, man, I don't want to have to live like a Christian. I still want to live the way I am living." Some people get hung up on some little doctrine they cannot accept by faith.

We had Rev. Massey of Pakistan in our home several weeks ago. He told about a very brilliant doctor who came to him and said, "If I could only believe that Jesus was the Son of God, I would accept Him as my Messiah." Rev. Massey reported, "God gave me the answer. I looked at that man and said to him, 'Do you believe the Koran?'" He replied in the affirmative. Rev. Massey queried, "Did you know that in the Koran Jesus Christ is spoken of as the Spirit of God and as one who was born of a virgin?" The man asserted that he did. "Well," said Rev. Massey, "If He is the Spirit of God, and He was born of a virgin, obviously a man couldn't be

His father. Isn't that correct?" "Why, of course," replied the doctor. "Well," said Rev. Massey, "Who is His father?" He answered the question, "God," and he accepted Christ.

Notice what the eighth verse says about those who allow Christ to continue being a stone of stumbling and a rock of offense to them. Such a person is appointed by almighty God to be separated eternally from Him in the place which the Bible calls hell.

Smiting Stone

In the fifth place, Jesus Christ is spoken of as the smiting stone cut without hands from the mountain. This takes us back to Daniel 2 and Nebuchadnezzar's dream. Part of the dream involved a great stone which would crush the world powers and become a great mountain and fill the whole earth. (See Dan. 2:34,35.)

Revelation 20 points out that Christ is the One who is going to fill the whole earth. It is He who will become the benevolent dictator of the affairs of man during His millennial kingdom.

Crushing Stone

The sixth and final picture of Christ is that of the Crushing Stone of Judgment. Christ is not only the power which crushes the unrighteous; but because men reject Christ they shall also come into judgment before God. "Therefore I say to you, the kingdom of God will be taken away from you, and be given to a nation producing the fruit of it. And he who falls on this stone will be broken to pieces; but on whomever it falls, it will scatter him like dust" (Matt. 21:43,44). This is the judgment described in Revelation 20:11-15, the judgment of the great white throne. Every Christ rejector is going to face this judgment.

CHRISTIANS ARE . . .

"But you are a chosen race, a royal priesthood, a holy nation, a people for God's own possession, that you may proclaim the excellencies of Him who has called you out of darkness into His marvelous light; for you once were not a people, but now you are the people of God; you had not received mercy, but now you have received mercy" (1 Pet. 2:9,10).

The Chosen Race

Simon Peter points out that we who name the name of Jesus as Saviour and Lord are a chosen race. God called the people of Israel to be His chosen race in order to perpetuate His ministry and to have fellowship with Him. The same thing is going to happen during the millennial period. The Jews, once again as a nation, are going to be elevated to this place of priority. In the meantime, in this age of grace, we as Christians are chosen to carry on His business and to enjoy fellowship on two levels: on the level of the human and on the level of the divine. John, the beloved apostle, has much to say about this. "What we have seen and heard we proclaim to you also, that you also may have fellowship with us; and indeed our fellowship is with the Father, and with His Son Jesus Christ. And these things we write, so that our joy may be made complete" (1 John 1:3,4). John is saying that he wants us to be happy Christians. He wants us to have this joy, this happiness, this exciting fellowship experience that we are offered both on the human and divine levels. Joy and happiness result in part from Christian fellowship. This warm and satisfying experience is marked by real love and friendship. "We know that we have passed out of death into life, because we love the brethren" (1 John 3:14). The brethren are our fellow Christians. Surely no one would argue with me when I make the statement that those we love are those with whom we want to associate. The believer who really loves his fellow Christians, which is a sign of true Christianity, is going to take advantage of every opportunity to have fellowship with them.

The only thing that is better than Christian fellowship on the human level is Christian fellowship on the divine level. We can have that fellowship anywhere, any time. As we read the Word of God, He speaks to us through the Word. As we get down on our knees in prayer, we speak to Him through prayer. Fellowship is established between us. When we have that fellowship continually, it enables us to take our minds, our attentions, our thoughts off of ourselves and place them on other people.

A young wife went into the hospital for brain surgery which proved to be cancer. She did not ask God to guide the hand of the surgeon that the operation would be successful. She didn't ask that her life be spared. She simply asked, whether she lived or died, that every member of her family would come to know Jesus Christ as Saviour. In answer to the prayers of this godly woman, her husband made his decision; and one by one the others are coming to know Christ as Saviour. She walks with the Lord because she is in constant fellowship with Him.

The Royal Priesthood

Every Christian is numbered among the "royal priesthood." "Royal" is the translation of the Greek word *basileion* which means "kingly." He is a part of a kingly priesthood. As we look back into the Old Testament, we discover that at the beginning God stipulated that the husband and father in the home should be the high priest. When He gave the Law at Mount Sinai, He gave the people of Israel an opportunity to become a kingdom of priests. "Now then, if you will indeed obey My voice and keep My covenant, then you shall be My own possession among all the peoples, for all the earth is Mine; and you shall be to Me a kingdom of priests. . ." (Exod. 19:5,6). If they would keep God's covenant, if they would be obedient to His voice as He had articulated the Law, then they could become a kingdom of priests.

The Law sets a perfect standard to which we as imperfect beings cannot adhere. Israel failed and God removed her opportunity for becoming a kingdom of priests. Instead, He selected Aaron and his family to be His priests. This was the situation until Good Friday when our Lord was crucified. During that experience there came one great moment when the veil of the Temple was ripped from top to bottom. From then on there has been no need for a select group of priests. From then on every believer became a priest, a part of God's royal priesthood. One of the most significant scriptural doctrines is that of the priesthood of all believers. The moment a person invites the Lord into his life to possess him, that individual becomes a priest unto God.

As priests we have a satisfying privilege and two

tremendous responsibilities. We have the privilege of going directly into the holy of holies in heaven itself to the Lord Jesus Christ, the High Priest, who is seated on the right hand of God the Father. As we go to Him in prayer we do not have to do so by fumbling beads, or by kneeling in front of a piece of statuary, or by praying through some ordained clergyman. We go directly to the Lord Jesus Christ, the High Priest of every Christian.

We have the responsibility of bringing others to Jesus Christ. God expects every Christian to confront others with the gospel, praying that the Holy Spirit will use that confrontation to bring conviction, conversion, redemption, reconciliation and transformation into their lives.

As priests unto God every believer has a second responsibility, "You also, as living stones, are being built up as a spiritual house for a holy priesthood, to offer up spiritual sacrifices acceptable to God through Jesus Christ" (1 Pet. 2:5). The apostle Paul wrote, "I urge you therefore, brethren, by the mercies of God, to present your bodies a living and holy sacrifice, acceptable to God, which is your spiritual service of worship" (Rom. 12:1). This simply means that in offering our bodies as living sacrifices, we offer our time and our talent to be directed by the Spirit of God in the implementing of His program in His church. Then after we have offered ourselves, we are to offer our substance, our tithes and offerings. The Bible says that the Christian who does not tithe is guilty of stealing from God. He is just as guilty of thievery as if he were to take some money out of the offering plate as it passed him in the morning service. We are guilty of stealing from God if we do not bring this sacrifice to Him (Mal. 3:9,10; Matt. 23:23). We are to first give ourselves and then our substance.

A Holy Nation

Not only are we a chosen race. Not only are we a kingly priesthood. But we as believers are a holy nation. The word "nation" is the Greek *laos* and it actually means people. We are a holy people. The word "holy" is the Greek word *hagios,* the same word from which we get our English word "saintly" or "saint." It also has other meanings. I like the one that William Barclay discusses, "The basic meaning of this word *hagios* is 'different.' The Christian has been chosen that he may be different from other men."[2] When he is in a group and someone begins to tell a dirty story, he excuses himself and leaves. When the ladies in the neighborhood get together and begin to rake over the coals the one neighbor who is not there, the Christian woman does her best to stop such conversation. When the kids in the classroom begin to cheat on an examination, the Christian guy and gal refuse to go along with it. Yes, Christians are different. They are dedicated to God's will and to God's service.

Probably one of the most familiar passages in the New Testament as far as evangelical Christians are concerned is, "For by grace you have been saved through faith; and that not of yourselves, it is the gift of God; not as a result of works, that no one should boast" (Eph. 2:8,9). But we stop at those two verses and don't go on to the next verse. "For we

71

are His workmanship, created in Christ Jesus for good works, which God prepared beforehand, that we should walk in them" (v. 10). Why did God offer salvation in grace to us which we can accept by faith? It is in order that our lives might be changed that we might be different people, that we become dedicated to the performance of good works.

A woman had not only threatened suicide but had attempted it. One night she was drunk and took some poison. She went to one of the other apartments and knocked on the door. When the people answered the door and saw her condition, they told her to go away. Then she knocked on the door of a family who belong to our church. They saw her condition, invited her in and took her to the hospital where she received the necessary treatment. She remained there for one week, and the family continued to minister to her. Finally, the wife led her to a saving knowledge of Jesus Christ and her life was transformed. She tells me now how happy she is to be in our church, and that she appreciates the messages God lays on my heart and on the hearts of the others who preach from our pulpit. She also states, "I am a new Christian, brought to the Lord through the untiring, loving efforts of Christian friends. I would truly have died if not for their unfailing love and patience." Dedicated unto good works: this is where we are to be different.

A Peculiar People

Last of all we are told that we are a people for God's own possession. Sometimes an article is valuable, not because of the article itself, but because of the person who has owned it. If I held in my hand the Bible that Martin Luther used when he led the Protestant Reformation and offered it for sale, I am sure that I could get two or three hundred thousand dollars for it. But his Bible is no different from the standpoint of the text from thousands of other Bibles that can be purchased for a very minimal amount. The difference is that Martin Luther once owned the Bible. This is the point that Peter is making here. You and I may not be very valuable as the world measures value. We may not be very high on the social ladder; we may not achieve much in our business; we may not be wealthy. But in the eyes of God we are valuable because we are possessed by Him. When a Christian realizes this, that Christian becomes very stable though the very foundations on which he has been standing are knocked from under him.

Footnotes
1. Barclay, *The Letters of James and Peter*, p. 231.
2. Barclay, *The Letters of James and Peter*, pp. 235-236.

5

---

1 Peter 2:11-25

THE NITTY-GRITTY OF EVERY DAY

"Beloved, I urge you as aliens and strangers to abstain from fleshly lusts, which wage war against the soul. Keep your behavior excellent among the Gentiles, so that in the thing in which they slander you as evildoers, they may on account of your good deeds, as they observe them, glorify God in the day of visitation" (1 Pet. 2:11,12).

The message of these verses can be summarized in three phrases: a loving approach, a negative and positive challenge, and a godly purpose.

A Loving Approach

Our attention is drawn to a loving approach. The strangers and pilgrims to whom he was making reference were Christians. A Christian is not a citizen of this world. He is a pilgrim, a stranger. The phrase "Beloved" is the translation of a Greek word, *agape-*

toi, which is the distinctive word for divine love. Peter is pointing out the fact that Christians are the object of God's divine love.

Notice Peter uses "I urge," not "I command." God does not make us do His will. We either do His will because we love Him or we refuse to do it. The Bible divides Christians into two categories: spiritual Christians and carnal Christians. The spiritual Christians are those who love Jesus Christ and are motivated by that love to serve Him day by day and implement His will in their lives. Carnal Christians accept Jesus as Saviour but refuse His Lordship.

A Negative and Positive Challenge

Next, our attention is drawn to a negative and positive challenge. The word "abstain" in the Greek means to eliminate completely. We are to eliminate completely those fleshly desires that we have because they are constantly warring against our souls. The apostle Paul gives us a much longer list of the works of the flesh in Galatians 5:19-21, and the first thing he mentions is adultery. Then he works his way through other evils such as uncleanness, hatred, strife, and so on.

Read carefully: "Those who practice such things shall not inherit the kingdom of God" (Gal. 5:21). Paul says that those who practice these things demonstrate the fact that they are not Christians regardless of what their profession is.

From the negative Peter moves to the positive, with the challenge that the Christian is to be honest in the sight of all men. His word is to be as good as his bond. He is to be a man of impeccable integrity.

78

There is a godly purpose in all of this. We find that purpose in the last part of the twelfth verse. The key to understanding the meaning of this is that word "visitation." Kenneth Wuest writes, "Whenever the word is used in the New Testament and translated 'visit' or 'visitation,' it refers to the visitation of God's mercy and grace. Here it refers to the day when, as Vincent puts it, 'God shall look upon these wanderers as a pastor over his flock, and shall become the overlooker or bishop of their souls. . . .' The good works of Christians, their beautiful and separated lives, are used of God as one of the means of bringing lost sinners to the Lord Jesus. When they are saved, God becomes the spiritual overseer of their souls. Then these sinners saved by grace will glorify Him because of the Christlike lives of certain Christians that caused them to want the Savior too."[1]

What is the godly purpose in our accepting this negative challenge and the positive challenge? It is that by our good works we might point others to Jesus Christ.

The story is told of a university student who wandered into a church one Sunday morning. When the preacher said, "Let us everyone bow his head and pray," this student didn't do that. He had not come to pray. As he looked around he noticed his professor of science who was praying. The student reports, "When I looked upon the face of my professor after the prayer, I saw reflected in there rest, peace and contentment—the very things that I had wanted and could not find." Years later the student told his professor, "Thank you for showing the way by your good works, and now as a medical missionary I am doing my best to show others the way." Showing others the way is not always easy.

THE CHRISTIAN AND GOVERNMENT

At eight o'clock one Sunday morning my doorbell rang. When I answered it, I found a young man who was a member of our church. He told me this story. "My outfit is going to shove off tomorrow for Viet Nam. I am not going with some of my buddies to Canada to escape it. I plan to be with my outfit. However, there is a question troubling me. You're my pastor and I want to ask you this question before I go. What great contribution will I make to my country by going to Viet Nam and dying for a cause we're not trying to win?"

This young man wanted me to discuss one of the basic issues of life—the responsibility and the relationship of a Christian to his government. Peter brings us face to face with this issue: "Submit yourselves for the Lord's sake to every human institution: whether to a king as the one in authority; or to governors as sent by him for the punishment of evildoers and the praise of those who do right. For such is the will of God that by doing right you may silence the ignorance of foolish men. Act as free men, and do not use your freedom as a covering for evil, but use it as bondslaves of God. Honor all men; love the brotherhood, fear God, honor the king" (1 Pet. 2:13-17).

There are four pivotal words I want to call to your attention, each of which suggests a very practical question. What is the *source* of government? What is the *purpose* of government? What is our *respon-*

sibility as Christians to our government? Do I as a Christian have a right to *disobey* my government?

Source of Government

What is the *source* of government? The answer to this question can be given in one word—God! Again and again the Scripture documents the truth of this.

"Let every person be in subjection to the governing authorities. For there is no authority except from God, and those which exist are established by God. Therefore he who resists authority has opposed the ordinance of God; and they who have opposed will receive condemnation upon themselves" (Rom. 13:1,2). Government did not come into being by accident. It is a creation of God; therefore, it is a most important institution.

Purpose of Government

What is the *purpose* of government? Peter infers that there are two: First, God recognized that man is inherently evil. If there is no check on his activities, if he doesn't have to answer to his peers for what he does, then anarchy will reign and the survival of the fittest will be the law of the land. God brought government into being to maintain law and order. Second, to provide an atmosphere and a climate in which the man who wants to devote himself to constructive purposes and develop himself to the fullest extent of his ability, may do so.

Paul infers another purpose of government in Romans 13:2. The inference here is that government exists for the purpose of administering justice. In Romans 13:4, Paul tells us that the government has

81

the right to use the sword in the administration of justice. Bear in mind that Rome used crucifixion for executing outsiders, but she used the sword for executing her own people. And those to whom Paul wrote the book of Romans understood this.

Responsibility to Government

What is our *responsibility* as Christians to our government? The Bible answers this in five ways. We have the responsibility of praying for our government. "I exhort therefore, that, first of all, supplications, prayers, intercessions, and giving of thanks, be made for all men; for kings, and for all that are in authority; that we may lead a quiet and peaceable life in all godliness and honesty"† (1 Tim. 2:1,2). I wonder if you have ever thought about this. Maybe we are not leading a quiet and peaceable life in all godliness and honesty because we do not take the time to pray not only for our government but for the other governments of the world.

We are to support our government with our taxes. "Render therefore to all their dues: tribute to whom tribute is due"† (Rom. 13:7).

You and I are to serve our government. "Put them in mind to be subject to principalities and powers, to obey magistrates, to be ready to every good work"† (Titus 3:1). Here Paul teaches that Christian citizens are to support those in power by good works.

We support our government by evangelizing. The Christian is the light of the world and the salt of the earth. The purpose of light is to dispel darkness and the purpose of salt is to preserve. The Christian dispels the darkness of superstition, evil and sin by his influence and he also preserves the good. The more people turn on to Jesus Christ, the more light will be shed and the more good will be preserved in our nation.

We are to honor our government. Vernon Grounds, in an unpublished essay, has written, "Honor means the recognition of the divine source of any state, glimpsing behind its faltering justice and misused authority the impeccable justice and equitable authority of God. . . . We must be able to distinguish between the office and the office holder." My mother used to say, "Harold, I may not like the office holder, but I respect and honor his office. If I don't like the one who is in the office I am going to pray him out of office, and work for someone who can occupy that place to the glory of God."

Obedience to Government

We are also to obey the government for wrath's sake. "For he is the minister of God to thee for good. But if thou do that which is evil, be afraid; for he beareth not the sword in vain: for he is the minister of God, a revenger to execute wrath upon him that doeth evil"† (Rom. 13:4).

We are to obey the government for conscience' sake. "Wherefore ye must needs be subject, not only for wrath, but also for conscience' sake"† (Rom. 13:5).

We are to obey our government for the Lord's sake. "For the Lord's sake, obey every law of your government: those of the king as head of the state, and those of the king's officers, for he has sent them to punish all who do wrong, and to honor those who do right. It is God's will that your good lives should silence those who foolishly condemn the Gospel without knowing what it can do for them, having never experienced its power. You are free from the law, but that doesn't mean you are free to do wrong. Live as those who are free to do only God's will at all times"†† (1 Pet. 2:13-16). The Christian who obeys the laws of the land has a good influence on others; his personal testimony for Christ is enhanced by his obedience.

This brings us to a very controversial question. Do I have the right to *disobey* my government? When the law of government and the law of God are in conflict, the Christian has no alternative but to obey the law of God. Christians will not always agree when there is a conflict between the law of God and the law of man. We are not to judge one another as to who is right. All judgment is in God's hands.

We have some illustrations in the Bible where people obeyed the law of God rather than the law of man. Consider the story of Shadrach, Meshach and Abednego. For obeying the law of God rather than man they were put in the fiery furnace. Daniel obeyed the law of God rather than the law of man and for that he was thrown into the den of lions. Stephen could have renounced his faith and saved his life but he refused to do so, and was stoned to death. It is interesting to note that all of these who obeyed God rather than men stayed and took their punishment. They didn't try to escape.

CHRIST, OUR EXAMPLE

Obeying includes the idea of servantship. Peter begins, "Servants be submissive to your masters with all respect. . . ." The word he used here is not the usual Greek word for servant, *doulos,* but rather *oiketai,* anyone living under the Roman government. Every man, woman and child of every nation that had been conquered by the armies of Rome was a part of the *oiketai.* They were all slaves to the Roman goveriment. William Barclay points out, "It was by no means only menial tasks which were performed by slaves. Doctors, teachers, musicians, actors, secretaries and stewards were slaves. In fact, all the work of Rome was done by slaves. By this time the Roman attitude was that there was no point in being master of the world and doing one's own work. Let the slaves do that, and let the citizens live in pampered idleness." [2]

In writing to these slaves Peter points out that they would have to serve two types of masters: a good and gentle master or what the *King James Version* calls a "froward" master. *Froward* is an Anglo-Saxon word which means adverse. A froward master was one who was adverse to Christ. He would go out of his way to make life miserable for any *oiketai* in his service who became Christians.

Now amazing as it may seem, Peter tells these servants that regardless of what master they had, for the sake of the Lord, they were to subject themselves in all fear and reverence to him. He then goes on to comment about the ones that had adverse masters. Let me paraphrase verse 19 for you: "If, as an abused and maltreated slave motivated by a consciousness of God's presence and will in your life, you endure the undeserved grief and suffering your evil master hands out, you are to be highly commended."

Peter calls to our attention an obvious comparison. "For what credit is there if, when you sin and are harshly treated, you endure it with patience? But if when you do what is right and suffer for it you patiently endure it, this finds favor with God. For you have been called for this purpose" (1 Pet. 2:20,21).

Consider how this applies to us today. Although we are not slaves, many times we find ourselves in a subservient position in business, in school, in the family or in the church. When those who are over us treat us unfairly, instead of striking back at them and wanting to get even with them, we are to take it in a Christlike, loving, patient, forgiving manner. For in doing this we become the Christian witnesses that Almighty God expects us to be.

Our Lord Jesus Christ is our example. "Since Christ also suffered for you, leaving you an example for you to follow in His steps" (v. 21). This word "example" is actually a picture word derived from the Greek *hupogrammos* which means "written under." It pictures words being given a child to copy both as a writing exercise and as a means of teaching him some great truth. Our Lord Jesus Christ is the perfect One to copy. He is the personification and epitome of all that is ethical, moral and spiritual.

Peter concludes this section by calling to our attention the perfection of Christ, the substitutionary death of the Saviour and the result of His death in the life of the believer. As he writes about the perfection of Christ he points out four important truths. He pictures Christ as perfect in the control of His activities, "who committed no sin" (v. 22). Christ was absolutely above reproach. What a high example that is for us to follow.

Christ was perfect in the control of His tongue. "Nor was any deceit found in His mouth; and while being reviled, He did not revile in return" (vv. 22,23).

He was perfect in the control of His temper. "While suffering, He uttered no threats" (v. 23). When those soldiers began to abuse Him, He didn't double up His fists and say, "I'm going to get even with you. You are going to rue the day you did this." Instead He prayed for them.

Finally, He was perfect in the commitment of Himself, "But kept entrusting Himself to Him who judges righteously" (v. 23). This is what God wants you and me to do when someone abuses or insults us. We are to take it, committing ourselves to Him who judges righteously. "Never take your own revenge, beloved, but leave room for the wrath of God, for it is written, 'Vengeance is Mine, I will repay, says the Lord'" (Rom. 12:19). The next time somebody insults you or tries to make life miserable for you, commit yourself to the Lord, take it graciously and see what happens.

CHRIST, OUR SAVIOUR

The central truth of the Christian faith is the substitutionary death of Christ for the believer. "He Himself bore our sins in His body on the cross, that we might die to sin and live to righteousness; for by His wounds you were healed" (v. 24). Christ died and poured out His precious blood on our behalf. When we invite Him into our lives, the death that He died becomes a substitutionary payment for the sins which we have committed, and by the stripes that He suffered we become whole people spiritually.

Peter calls to our attention the result of the substitutionary atonement in the life of the believer (v. 25). Let me paraphrase it for you. "Before Christ came into your life you were like a sheep that was not following his shepherd. You were right on the precipice of hell. But then Christ came into your life. Now you have returned unto the shepherd and the bishop of your souls." The word *bishop* is the Greek word *episcopos* which means an "overseer," a "provider," a "guide." Here Peter is emphasizing a point that is most assuring to the discerning Christian. Christ is the "Bishop-Shepherd" of every believer. As such, He provides for him. He gives him guidance and counsel, and meets his every need.

Footnotes

1. Wuest, *First Peter in the Greek New Testament*, p. 60.
2. Barclay, *The Letters of James and Peter*, p. 249.

6

---

1 Peter 3:1-12

RELATIONSHIP OF WIFE TO HUSBAND

In the first 7 verses of chapter 3, Peter spells out what God expects of every wife in her relationship to her husband, and contrariwise, what He expects of every husband in his relationship with his wife. In the first 6 verses he indicates the wife's duties and in verse 7 the obligations of the husband.

Submissive

In examining the first section we discover that there are six requirements a wife is expected to fulfill. The first of these has to do with her being submissive to her husband. Peter wrote, "In the same way, you wives, be submissive to your own husbands" (v. 1). This does not mean that a wife is to be a slave to her husband; it does not mean that his every whim is to be her supreme command. It does mean that she is not to be competitive with him, that she recognizes that she has been created to be his helpmeet.

A submissive wife fits into her husband's plans. We have a wonderful illustration of this in verse 6. "Thus Sarah obeyed Abraham, calling him lord, and you have become her children if you do what is right without being frightened by any fear." In chapter 12 of Genesis we are told that God called Abraham to leave the community where he was and settle in a country about which he knew nothing. The Bible tells us that Sarah, his wife, went with him. I can just see some wives reacting to this same situation today. "I'm not going one step with you, Buster, until you tell me what our security is going to be, where we are going to live, and what the details are of your job." They are not willing to fit into their husbands' plans.

2. **Faithful**

The wife is to be faithful to her husband. Verse 1 says, "be submissive to your own husbands." You are to be faithful to your *own* husband, not somebody else's.

3. **No Nagger**

The next requirement is a negative one. She is not to nag her husband. "Even if any of them are disobedient to the word they may be won without a word by the behavior of their wives" (v. 1). Unfortunately there are many well-intentioned Christian women with unsaved husbands who are literally driving them away from the Lord because of their relentless nagging. The more they nag, the further their husbands get away from the Lord.

Chaste and Respectful 4.

The wife is to be both chaste and respectful, "as they observe your chaste and respectful behavior" (v. 2). "Chaste" comes from the Greek *agnen,* and it means "pure." The wife is to have the reputation of being the epitome of morality and purity, and she is to have respect for her husband.

Beautiful Inside 5.

The final requirement has to do with the way in which a woman seeks to make herself beautiful. There is a negative aspect to this, and a positive one. The negative is described for us in the third verse, "And let not your adornment be external only—braiding the hair, and wearing gold jewelry, and putting on dresses." Don't let your beauty be simply a matter of outward appearance. The Roman women had a custom of making their coiffures very extreme. Clement of Alexandria describes women who piled tier upon tier until they nearly worshiped that which they piled upon their heads. Peter said, "You are not to be that extreme." Then he talks about the women not wearing gold jewelry. This does not mean they were not to wear any jewelry but rather that a woman is not to put on so much that she lights up like a Christmas tree. Finally, he talks about the dresses of the women by saying their wardrobes were not to be their god. I know women who spend more time thinking and talking about dresses and what they are going to wear than they do reading their Bible and speaking to others about Jesus Christ. Solomon has something to say about this too, "A beautiful woman lacking discretion and modesty is like a fine gold ring in a pig's snout"†† (Prov. 11:22). This doesn't mean that a wife should not make herself attractive to her husband. The wife is to be attractive, yes, but in discretion and in modesty.

In verses 4 and 5 Peter discusses a wife's inner beauty. He writes, "But let it be the hidden person of the heart, with the imperishable quality of a gentle and quiet spirit, which is precious in the sight of God. For in this way in former times the holy women also, who hoped in God, used to adorn themselves, being submissive to their own husbands." In effect he is saying, "The holy women of old developed a quiet, gentle spirit which is imperishable, and so they became beautiful on the inside."

The Results

Look again at verse 1. Peter promises that if a wife is married to an unsaved man and she practices all six of these responsibilities, her husband will someday become a Christian. As a boy, I remember a man in prayer meeting saying, "I was an alcoholic. When I'd come home my wife would badger me and make life so miserable I could hardly wait to get drunk again. But one night she met me with loving arms, sat me in a chair, gave me coffee, and put me to bed without saying a word. She did this every night for two weeks until I couldn't stand it. 'Why don't

94

you nag me instead of loving me?' I cried. She answered, 'I can't because God loves you.' I couldn't take it anymore. I invited Christ into my heart. We now have a Christ-centered home, and God is blessing."

RELATIONSHIP OF HUSBAND TO WIFE

In the seventh verse Peter turns his guns on the men. "You husbands likewise, live with your wives in an understanding way, as with a weaker vessel, since she is a woman; and grant her honor as a fellow-heir of the grace of life, so that your prayers may not be hindered." Peter recognized a reciprocal relationship in marriage. It is not one-sided. Marriage is a union of two and each is important. William Barclay in commenting on this said, "Any marriage in which all the privileges are on one side and all the obligations are on the other is bound to be an imperfect marriage with every chance of failure."[1]

The idea of marriage having any reciprocity was foreign to the Roman mind. A woman in those days had no rights. She was nothing more than a slave.

Understand Her

Peter strongly counters this concept by outlining two responsibilities for husbands and then implying a promise. The first responsibility is expressed in the first part of verse 7: husbands should live with their wives in an "understanding way." Some men have the old-fashioned idea that they are the lord and master, and the wife is the vassal to do his bidding. This is as far from the truth as the east is from the west.

Recognize Her Spiritual Equality

This brings us to the second responsibility. The husband is to recognize his wife as a fellow-heir of the grace of life. She is his equal spiritually, and because of this he should plan with her, talk with her, and pray with her about all of his problems, prospects and desires. He is to have no secrets from her. She is his life's companion and partner.

The Promise

The last part of verse 7 contains an implied promise to the husband who meets these requirements, "that your prayers may not be hindered." Peter is saying to the husband, "If you are out of fellowship with your wife because of some wrongdoing on your part, you are out of fellowship with God and therefore He will not hear your prayers."

OUR RELATIONSHIP TO ONE ANOTHER

Most of the people in the United States of America, even those who have their names on church rolls, are more concerned about doing their own thing than they are about doing the will of God. This is resulting in the moral, spiritual, and ethical declination of our country.

You ask, "What can we as Christians do about it?" Peter answers this for us in verses 8-12. He begins with the words, "To sum up." He is saying, "I have discussed with you the relationship between a Christian slave and his master, and the relationship between a Christian wife and her husband. Now I want to sum it all up by discussing with you the relationship that should exist between Christians in general." Then he goes on to list six virtues that all believers are to put into practice.

Harmonious

The first is harmony. He writes in verse 8, "To sum up, let all be harmonious." This is a translation of the Greek word, *homophrones*. It literally means "to be of the same mind." Here Simon Peter is pleading that you and I get along with one another as Christian brothers and sisters, that we be united in the Spirit.

Again and again throughout the Bible we are told as Christians that we are to live in harmony; we are to be united. This does not mean that we are going to see eye to eye on every biblical doctrine. We are not! It is inevitable that we disagree on some doctrines, but when we disagree, we are not to be disagreeable. We are to maintain the unity of the body by recognizing that even though we may have a difference of opinion in peripheral matters, we are one in our love for Christ and our desire to serve Him.

Sympathetic

Now look at the second virtue. Not only are we to live harmoniously, but we are to be sympathetic. This comes from the Greek *sumpatheis,* which means "to have a fellow feeling for." Romans 12:15 explains what is involved in this. We are to rejoice with those who rejoice and weep with those who weep. It is very easy to carry out the second part of that, and very difficult for the first. It is so easy to weep with those who weep; our very natures cry out for this. But if we are in the same business as somebody else and we see him getting ahead, it is most difficult to rejoice with him in his rejoicing.

Brotherly

The third virtue is expressed by the word "brotherly," a translation of *philadelphoi* from which the city of Philadelphia derives its name. It actually means "brotherly love." Our relationship, one with the other, should be characterized by this significant virtue.

In the story of Jonathan and David we have a beautiful picture of how this works. From the very inception of their relationship Jonathan had a profound love for the sweet singer of Israel. "The soul of Jonathan was knit to the soul of David, and Jonathan loved him as himself" (1 Sam. 18:1). That must have been most difficult for Jonathan. He by right of inheritance looked forward to occupying the throne, but he knew this was for David. However, he loved David as he loved himself. And this love was reciprocated. When David learned that Saul and Jonathan had died, he sang a lament over them in which he expressed his great love for them. (See 2 Sam. 1:26,27.) David and Jonathan had that brotherly love for one another that God expects each and every one of us to have for each other.

Kindhearted

In the next place, Simon Peter tells us that Christians are to be kindhearted. This is a translation of the Greek word *eusplagchnoi* which means "compassionate, having pity."

William Barclay, in commenting on the significance of this, wrote, "Pity is the very essence of God; compassion is of the very being of Jesus Christ; a pity so great that God sent His only Son to die for men, a compassion so intense that it took Christ to the cross. There can be no Christianity without compassion."[2]

Humble

In the fifth place Peter informs us that in our relationship one to the other, we are to be humble in spirit. Someone has said that humility is that virtue which, when you think you have it, you have lost it. Meditate on that for a minute.

An egocentric is avoided by everyone who knows him. Simon Peter recognized this. Under the inspiration of the Holy Spirit, he points out that if you and I are going to be effective as a force for God and for good, we must develop the spirit of humility.

We can develop humility by recognizing our dependence upon God. None of us is a self-made man, regardless of how much money he may have, how popular he may be, or what standing he may enjoy on the social ladder. We are completely dependent upon God. Anytime He desires, He can withdraw the breath of life from us. When we recognize that we are completely dependent upon Him for everything we have, humility is the inevitable result.

Comparison is often a humbling experience. As individuals, the One with whom we are to compare ourselves is the Lord Jesus Christ. We are told in 1 Peter 2:21 that He is our example. Paul, in talking about Christ said, "Let this mind be in you, which

99

was also in Christ Jesus: who, being in the form of God, thought it not robbery to be equal with God: but made himself of no reputation, and took upon him the form of a servant, and was made in the likeness of men: And being found in fashion as a man, he humbled himself, and became obedient unto death, even the death of the cross"† (Phil. 2:5-8). You talk about a humbling experience—compare yourself with Christ at this point. If you tend to be cocky, this will knock it out of you.

The individual that God uses in His service is the humble person. A young man who was a rather unlikely prospect applied as an assistant missionary in China. When the board interviewed him they said, "We can't send you out as an assistant because you do not qualify, but we can commission you as a servant to another missionary if you are willing to work on that level." Consider this young man's reply: "Well, sirs, if the gentlemen don't think me fit to be a missionary, I will go as a servant. I am willing to be a hewer of wood or a drawer of water or do anything to help the cause of my heavenly Master." That young man became Dr. Milne, one of the greatest missionaries that ever served in China. But he went out simply as a servant.

Forgiving Spirit

If you and I are going to have the relationship one to the other which God expects us to have, we must have a forgiving spirit. This is what verse 9 is all about: "Not returning evil for evil, or insult for insult, but giving a blessing instead; for you were called for the very purpose that you might inherit

100

a blessing." What Peter is saying is, "Instead of returning evil for evil or insult for insult, when somebody does something wrong to us or when somebody insults us, we are to give that person a blessing, and the only way we can do so is to forgive him." Notice the reciprocal arrangement. If we will forgive those who insult us and do evil against us, thereby bestowing a blessing upon them, God will bless us in like manner. If we refuse this forgiveness, God will not forgive us, thereby forcing us to live with a guilty conscience. If we extend this forgiveness, then the Almighty will do the same and our consciences will be clear and free.

Forgiveness has the dimension of limitlessness and the dimension of forgetfulness. Limitlessness means simply that there will be no limit to the number of times we are willing to forgive one another. Simon Peter said to Jesus, "How often shall my brother sin against me and I forgive him? Up to seven times?" (Matt. 18:21,22). Jesus answered, "Seventy times seven." He did not mean 490 times. He meant that we should keep on forgiving him as often as he offends us. Our willingness to forgive must be limitless.

Then there is to be the dimension of forgetfulness. I have heard people say, "I will forgive, but I won't forget." You cannot forgive without forgetting. In Micah 7:19 the prophet says God buries our sins beneath the depths of the sea. What a picture of forgetfulness that is. Isaiah 38:17 tells us that when God forgives us, He puts our sins behind His back so that He cannot see them. Psalm 103:12 states, "As far as the east is from the west, so far has He removed

101

our transgressions from us." That's forgetfulness!

In verses 10-12 Peter summarizes that which he has said in verses 8 and 9. He writes, "For let him who means to love life and see good days refrain his tongue from evil and his lips from speaking guile. And let him turn away from evil and do good; let him seek peace and pursue it. For the eyes of the Lord are upon the righteous, and His ears attend to their prayer, but the face of the Lord is against those who do evil."

There is a choice that Christians have to make. We can either decide to allow Christ to be the Lord of our lives, with the Holy Spirit implementing these six virtues, or we can decide to be content with the salvation God has given us, having no desire to be involved in serving Him. And if we do that, Simon Peter tells us we will come under the judgment of God.

Footnotes
1. Barclay, *The Letters of James and Peter*, p. 264.
2. Barclay, *The Letters of James and Peter*, p. 269.

7

---

1 Peter 3:13-22

CHRISTIAN'S RELATIONSHIP TO UNBELIEVERS

Peter opens this section by saying, "And who is there to harm you if you prove zealous for what is good? But even if you should suffer for the sake of righteousness, you are blessed. And do not fear their intimidation, and do not be troubled." *The Living Bible* translates this so clearly it becomes self-explanatory, "Usually no one will hurt you for wanting to do good. But even if they should, you are to be envied, for God will reward you for it."††

Acknowledge Christ as Master and Lord

Peter then calls to our attention a very practical and important commandment. "But sanctify Christ as Lord in your hearts, always being ready to make a defense to every one who asks you to give an account for the hope that is in you." "Sanctify" is a translation of the Greek word *hagiasate,* meaning "to set apart." In this particular reference, the verb is in the aorist tense which in the Greek language means a once-and-for-all action. Simon Peter is saying, "In your heart, in the inner recesses of your being, once and for all you set Christ apart as the Lord of your life, the supreme object of your worship and service. Everything else must be secondary."

If you think this is a rather stringent requirement, let me ask you to look at the way in which the Lord Jesus Himself expresses this same idea. These verses describe our Lord's statements during the zenith of His popularity. "Now great multitudes were going along with Him; and He turned and said to them, 'If anyone comes to me, and does not hate his own father and mother and wife and children and brothers and sisters, yes, and even his own life, he cannot be My disciple. Whoever does not carry his own cross and come after Me cannot be My disciple'" (Luke 14:25-27). We must look at this closely because Christ is not telling us objectively that we are to hate our loved ones and our own life. The word "hate" as He uses it here is a word of comparison. He is saying our love for Him, our involvement in serving Him, and our capitulation of ourselves to Him should be so complete that when our love for our family, our friends and our own life is compared to it, that love seems as hatred.

It is not enough for us to acknowledge Christ as Saviour. I am convinced that most of the members of the average evangelical church have acknowledged Christ as Saviour. But I am also convinced that most of the members of these churches have never acknowledged Christ as their Master and Lord. Christ must be Lord of all in our lives or He is not going to be Lord at all. We must give Him everything. And if we fail at this point then our testimony for Him will be impotent and ineffective. We are to sanctify Christ as Lord of our lives once and for all, and be constantly ready to defend our faith when someone challenges us. The word "to defend" comes from the Greek word *apologian* which means "to make a defense." An apology is not feeling sorry for something you have done: an apology is a defense of what you have done. Seminarians study Christian apologetics, the defense of the gospel. We are told that each and every one of us should be a Christian apologist. We must be ready to defend our faith at a moment's notice.

The reason that most of us are ineffective is that we don't know how to wield the only weapon God will use in defeating the adversary, the Bible. We are to know the Word of God, and with that, we are to defend our faith.

Defend Our Faith by Gentleness

In the second part of verse 15 Peter informs us that our defense of the faith is to be characterized by gentleness. This is the Greek word, *prautetos*, which means "meekness." *Prautetos* includes the ideas of self-control and kindness. When we are defending our faith, we are to do it with self-control and kindness. That is hard because usually our antagonists will do their best to make us mad. They know that if they succeed in this they will win the battle.

In verse 16 Peter discusses the result of this type of apology. Notice the first part of the verse, "and keep a good conscience." This is an erroneous translation. It should be translated, "and having a good conscience." Peter was saying, "As long as you implement this command in the spirit of meekness and respect you will have a clear conscience."

Possibility of Suffering

Now look closely at verse 17, "For it is better, if God should will it so, that you suffer for doing what is right rather than for doing what is wrong." It may be God's will that you and I suffer for our faith. If it ever comes, we are to remember that it is better to suffer for doing good than for doing evil. The first brings God's blessings; the second His judgment. Christ is the prime example of this.

PURPOSE OF CHRIST'S DEATH

Christ's death was neither by accident nor by the will of man, but by the will of God, "For Christ also died for sins" (1 Pet. 3:18). The main purpose for the coming of Christ into the world was to die and conquer death that man might live. Paul wrote, "Who was delivered up because of our transgressions, and was raised because of our justification" (Rom. 4:25).

Christ's death was a once-and-for-all action, never to be repeated. When He died on Calvary's cross that death was sufficient to provide eternal salvation for every human being of every generation. In the Old Testament the high priest went into the holy of holies once a year to offer a blood sacrifice to atone both for his sins and the sins of the people.

But not so with the eternal High Priest, our Lord Jesus Christ. (See Heb. 9:24-28.) The apostle Paul said, "Knowing that Christ, having been raised from the dead, is never to die again; death no longer is master over Him. For the death that He died, He died to sin, once for all; but the life that He lives, He lives to God" (Rom. 6:9,10).

Peter calls our attention to the fact that the purpose of Christ's death is that He might bring us to God. "For Christ also died for sins once for all, the just for the unjust, in order that He might bring us to God" (v. 18). The verb "to bring" is the Greek word *prosago* from which we get two nouns, *prosagoge* which means "the right of access" and *prosagogeus* which means "introducer" or "the giver of access." During the days when Greece was flourishing every king had a prosagogeus or an introducer. No one could have access to him except through the prosagogeus. Christ is the Father's prosagogeus. It is through Him and only through Him that a man has access to the Almighty. Jesus Himself made this clear when He said, "I am the way, and the truth, and the life; no one comes to the Father, but through Me" (John 14:6).

After discussing the death of Christ, the Big Fisherman writes concerning the urgency of salvation. This brings us face to face with the most difficult passage in the entire Bible. Look very closely: "having been put to death in the flesh, but made alive in the spirit; in which also He went and made proclamation to the spirits now in prison, who once were disobedient, when the patience of God kept waiting in the days of Noah, during the construction of the ark" (1 Pet.

109

3:18,19,20). Many and varied are the interpretations of this. I have read a number of theories which come from very competent, evangelical scholars.

There are those who claim that this is a reference to the day of Noah, and that the preaching that took place was done by Christ through Noah to the people of his age. But the text indicates that it was after He had been put to death in the flesh that He went to those people and preached.

There are those who believe that it wasn't Jesus who did the preaching but that it was Enoch. We are told in the book of Enoch that Enoch went down to the place where the fallen angels were being kept for eternity and announced to them that their doom was sealed. The book of Enoch is not part of the canon, and furthermore Enoch does not appear in any of the Greek manuscripts.

There are those who believe that Christ went into Hades and preached to those in its upper compartment. They interpret Scripture to indicate that there are two compartments of Hades—one reserved for the lost and the other for those who would some day be saved. According to this theory, the Lord Jesus Christ told the people in the "saved" compartment that their redemption was complete, that He had paid the penalty for their sin. Then He led them out of there and into the presence of God. But as we look at the text it is difficult to see all of this.

Other well-meaning people love God and everyone else so much that they forget God is the God of justice as well as the God of mercy. These people teach that the Lord Jesus Christ went into both compartments of Hades and announced that He had paid

110

the penalty for their sin by His death on the cross; therefore, He was giving them a second chance to acknowledge Him as Saviour and Lord. This is a subtle form of universalism. The New Testament cries out, "No! No! No! NO!" This cannot possibly be true. "Between us and you there is a great chasm fixed, in order that those who wish to come over from here to you may not be able, and that none may cross over from there to us" (Luke 16:26).

Some reputable evangelical scholars take the position that between the time of His crucifixion and resurrection, Jesus went to Tartaurus, the place reserved for the condemned angels. There He preached to them that their doom had been sealed. But as we look at the text we are told that Christ preached to those who were disobedient during the days of Noah. In Genesis 6:3 God declares, "My Spirit shall not strive with man forever." Not angels! But men!

I think it is best to take this passage literally. Noah, while he was building the ark, pled with the people of his day to follow the leadership of almighty God who was most patient with them. He gave them ample opportunity to do the thing that He wanted them to do. But the time came when God's spirit would no longer strive with them. They sinned away their day of opportunity. Only eight entered that ark and were saved. The others were lost. Peter tells us that to these who were lost, Jesus went and preached between the time of His crucifixion and His resurrection. To be consistent with the Word of God, the only message that He could have preached was that He had completed redemption; therefore, their doom was sealed. They had no second chance.

URGENCY OF SALVATION

As we look at this, it suggests to us the urgency of salvation. Eternity is forever and there are no second chances. God is dealing with people now just as He did the antediluvians (those who lived before the flood). He is patient. He is giving them time. He is actually sparing their lives so that they may have additional opportunities for embracing His plan for their lives. But this will not always be. Wise, therefore, is the man who realizes the urgency of this matter and takes care of it immediately.

Simon Peter next calls to our attention Noah's ark and baptism; he writes, "In which a few, that is, eight persons, were brought safely through the water" (v. 20). The ark is an excellent illustration of the way in which God saves because it is an almost perfect type of Christ. As we examine the historical circumstances in which the ark was built we discover that it was the divinely chosen means of saving the human race. It was God's idea to build that ark, not Noah's. He came to Noah and announced what He was going to do. Christ, like that ark, is the divinely appointed means of saving man, and that appointment was made long before man was ever thought of or heard of. He was selected before the foundation of the world to become the means by which the human race should be saved.

Secondly, we look at the ark and discover that it was the exclusive means of salvation. So it is with Jesus Christ. He is the triune God's only appointed means of salvation.

We learn that the ark took the beating that those inside the ark would have taken had they been on the outside. The Bible in describing the flood says that God let the water come up from the depths and He poured it down from above so that the ark was caught in a pincer movement of tremendous water pressure. Then as the flood became most intense. the water began to wash debris against the sides of the ark. Yes, the ark took the beating that the people on the inside would have taken had they been on the outside. What a picture this is of the crucifixion of our Lord Jesus Christ. He took the beating that you and I deserve that we might have life abundant and everlasting.

In the fourth place, entrance into the ark was voluntary. God invited Noah and his family to come into the ark. They did not have to obey; their action in doing so was by faith on a voluntary basis. So it is in every man's relationship with Jesus Christ. God does not coerce anybody to accept Jesus as Saviour. The invitation is, "Him that cometh unto Me I will in no wise cast out." Every man that comes to Jesus Christ must do so by faith on a voluntary basis.

In the fifth place entrance into the ark was free. God didn't ask for an admission ticket; it was free. So it is in our relationship with Jesus Christ. Paul wrote, "For by grace are ye saved through faith; and that not of yourselves: it is the gift of God: not of works, lest any man should boast"† (Eph. 2:8,9).

Last of all we discover that after the people were in the ark God shut the door, and He was in complete charge. He kept them in safety throughout that flood until the moment came when they could walk out of that ark and be on dry land once again. What

113

a picture this is of the security that Christ provides for every one of us. Once we are in Christ Jesus we are there until we are presented to Him face to face in eternity. Paul said, "For I am confident of this very thing, that He who began a good work in you will perfect it until the day of Christ Jesus" (Phil. 1:6). When you and I accept Christ as Saviour, God the Holy Spirit comes into our lives. He begins the good work of redemption in us and continues it until the day of Christ, until the day when He returns for His own. (See 1 Thess. 4:13-18.) You talk about security; that's it. Not only on the time level, but on the eternal level.

Peter's next illustration of salvation is baptism. "Corresponding to that, baptism now saves you—not the removal of dirt from the flesh" (v. 21). It is not the act of baptism itself that saves you, it is something else. What is it? He answers, "but an appeal to God for a good conscience," or a better translation of that would be, "but the pledge of a good conscience toward God." The word "pledge" is a Greek word *eperotema* which is actually a description of what happened during a business transaction. Two businessmen would enter into a deal. The seller would make his proposition to the buyer. The buyer would then consider what he had to say, and based upon that consideration, he would either accept or reject the deal. If he accepted it, the buyer would stand and say, "I pledge that I am going to live according to the terms of this contract." He did this before witnesses, and that sealed the contract. Now keep this in mind as we consider baptism.

Basically baptism is to symbolize the death, burial

and resurrection of Jesus Christ. When Christ asked John the Baptist to baptize Him, He said to him, "It is fitting for us to fulfill all righteousness" (Matt. 3:15). When you and I are presented the gospel of the Lord Jesus Christ we can either accept it or reject it. There is no halfway measure, there is no neutral ground; we either say "yes" or "no." If we say "yes" we seal the contract by being baptized. In being baptized we are saying to the world, "I accept the terms of the contract which God has made, namely, that I am saved by faith in the death, burial and resurrection of Jesus Christ. This is my pledge of a good conscience that I have accepted Christ."

TRIUMPH OF CHRIST

Last of all, Peter calls to our attention the triumph of Christ. This he does in verses 21,22 by zeroing in on our Lord's resurrection and ascension and the subjection of angels, authorities and powers to Himself. We may be called upon someday to suffer for our faith. But we are not to be really concerned about it; for if we are faithful we shall share in Christ's victorious experiences. After all, we are His brothers and sisters and joint-heirs with Him of heaven's riches. (See Rom. 8:17.)

In 1 Peter 4:12-19 Simon Peter summarizes this whole concept. *The Living Bible* translates it; "Dear friends, don't be bewildered or surprised when you go through the fiery trials ahead, for this is no strange, unusual thing that is going to happen to you. Instead, be really glad—because these trials will make you partners with Christ in his suffering, and afterwards you will have the wonderful joy of sharing his glory in that coming day when it will be displayed. Be happy if you are cursed and insulted for being a Christian, for when that happens the Spirit of God will come upon you with great glory. Don't let me hear of your suffering for murdering or stealing or making trouble or being a busybody and prying into other people's affairs. But it is no shame to suffer for being a Christian. Praise God for the privilege of being in Christ's family and being called by his wonderful name! For the time has come for judgment, and it must begin first among God's own children. And if even we who are Christians must be judged, what terrible fate awaits those who have never believed in the Lord? If the righteous are barely saved, what chance will the godless have? So if you are suffering according to God's will, keep on doing what is right and trust yourself to the God who made you, for he will never fail you."††

8

---

1 Peter 4:1-19

First Peter 4:1-11 centers around four pivotal words: (1) Command (2) Consequence (3) Concern and (4) Consummation.

COMMAND

The command is stated in two words found in verse 1, "Arm yourself." The Greek word here is "opil-sasthe" which pictures a Greek warrier putting on his heaviest armor for maximum protection.

As Christians we are to arm ourselves with the same purpose which motivated the Saviour to suffer and die on Calvary. And His purpose was to do the will of the Father and finish His work. Therefore, says Peter, "Since Christ has suffered in the flesh, arm yourselves also with the same purpose."

That purpose was stated also by Jesus Himself when He told His disciples, "My meat is to do the will of Him who sent Me, and to accomplish His work" (John 4:34).

119

Peter reminds us that as Christians we are to arm ourselves with that same resolution to do God's will in our lives even if doing so means suffering and even martyrdom.

He then goes on to write that "he who has suffered in the flesh has ceased from sin, so as to live the rest of the time in the flesh no longer for the lusts of men, but for the will of God" (vv. 1,2). Peter is not saying here that such Christians have reached the place of sinless perfection. That is not what the phrase "has ceased from sin" means. He affirms that, like Christ, those who have made the will of God their life objective and who have been persecuted for it are no longer dominated by sin. They have conquered the lust of the flesh; their thing now is the doing of the will of God and His will only.

Peter is writing in verse 3 to those who—prior to their conversion—spent all their time in sensual pleasure: "You have had enough in the past of evil things the godless enjoy—sex sin, lust, getting drunk, wild parties, drinking bouts, and the worship of idols—which lead to other terrible sins."

The message comes through loud and clear if you are still doing these things, forget it; you are not a Christian! Your so-called conversion experience was simply an emotional jag; you are still on your way to hell.

Peter's inspired message applies to all of us today. He says what Jesus already said: "Wherefore by their fruits you shall know them" (Matt. 7:20). Professing Christians who booze it up, play loose with their marriage vows, and worship the idols of money, pleasure, and lust are nothing but hypocrites! Unless there is a change and real conversion they will one day hear the Master say, "Depart from me, ye that work iniquity; I never knew you" (Matt. 7:23).

CONSEQUENCE

In verses 4 and 5, Peter calls to our attention the consequence of an individual implementing the command to arm himself with the same purpose that Christ had for His life. Simply stated this individual will no longer involve himself in a life of dissipation. And his former friends, says Peter, "are surprised" that he does "not run with them into the same excess of dissipation" (v. 4).

The verb "to run" is the Greek word "suntrekontown" meaning to "run in a pack," a word picture of the worldly crowd running and sinning together today. Like packs of animals they move from one bar to another, from one "key" club to another, seemingly rejoicing on their way to hell and taking solace in knowing they are not going alone.

Romans 1:26-32 describes them and their fate perfectly, "That is why God let go of them and let them do all these evil things . . . They were fully aware of God's death penalty for these crimes, yet they went right ahead and did them anyway, and encouraged others to do them, too."

Yes, this crowd will be surprised that one from their number will no longer associate himself as a Christian with their immoral pursuits. But do not miss a subtlety here. While the believer will not indulge himself with them, he will still remain friendly with individuals in the group, always looking for an opportunity to share his faith with them. He will avoid a "holier than thou attitude," recognizing that but for the grace of God he would still be running with the pack.

But Peter also warns him that his former crowd will not only be surprised at him, but they will also mock him and seek to make his life miserable. In the face of this, the believer is to remember and practice vigorously Romans 12:19, "Avenge not yourselves, but rather give place unto wrath, for it is written, 'Vengeance is mine; I will repay, saith the Lord.'"

And as Peter writes in verse 5, "They shall give account to Him (Jesus Christ) who is ready to judge the living and the dead." The "they" in this statement are those who have turned their backs on God's plan for their lives, rejected Jesus Christ and have run with the godless pack. And Christ will judge them at the judgment of the great white throne graphically described in Revelation 20:11-15.

CONCERN

In verse 6, Peter calls to our attention this fact: God is concerned that people avoid the horrors of this final judgment. This is the main purpose for the preaching of the gospel: "For the gospel has for this purpose been preached even to those who are dead, that though they are judged in the flesh as men, they may live in the spirit according to the will of God."

Here Peter remembers that the gospel was preached to many he knew who are now dead. And two things happened to them: first, they had been judged in the flesh as men and experienced death. In Hebrews 9:27 we are told that "it is appointed unto men once to die." This is because of Adam's sin. And if the Lord delays His coming this is the judgment that awaits us all.

Second, those who experienced death in the flesh are now living in the Spirit according to the will of God. In other words through the preaching of the gospel they accepted Christ as Saviour and are now absent from their bodies but at home with the Lord (2 Cor. 5:8). The inference is that they are awaiting the day when the Lord shall return and raise their bodies from the dead, making them incorruptible and reuniting them with their spirits (1 Thess. 4:13-18).

As in Peter's day, God is still concerned that people avoid the final judgment of the great white throne. So he has commissioned us as Christians to share our faith with those who aren't.

How are we doing?

CONSUMMATION

Peter declares in verse 7 that "the end of all things is at hand." By "all things" he means two things: first, the Christian faces the possibility of death every moment of his life; and second, the Lord may come at any moment thereby bringing to an end this age of grace. And Peter implies that we are to live every day as if it were the last day of our lives.

Peter then uses the word "therefore," as if to say, "Because of this, God expects you to do certain things." Altogether there are four things: prayer, love, hospitality and spiritual gifts.

The first has to do with prayer. Peter writes, "Be of sound judgment and sober spirit for the purpose of prayer." Let me paraphrase this for you: "Evaluate things in the light of time and also in the light of eternity. And avoid excessive frivolity, being calm in spirit as you regularly approach the Lord in prayer."

I can assure you that if we do this, we will experience such spiritual power that we will accomplish miracles for God.

The second has to do with love. Peter writes in verse 8, "Above all, keep fervent in your love for one another, because love covers a multitude of sins." "Above all" means "first in order of importance." Peter is saying that we should give top priority to being fervent in our love for one another, recognizing that love doesn't publicize the sins of others; instead it forgives and forgets them.

The word "fervent" comes from the Greek "ektenes" and it means "stretching out as a runner stretches out." As a runner nears the end of the race he will stretch out with every fibre of his being in an effort to break the tape before his opponents do. This is the way you and I should stretch ourselves out in love one for the other, extending ourselves to the maximum in meeting each other's needs.

The third has to do with hospitality. In verse 9 we read, "Be hospitable to one another without complaint." The Greek word translated hospitable is "philxenoi," meaning "be friendly to strangers." Not only are we to love our fellow Christians whom we know, but we are to be friendly to those whom we do not know even to entertaining them in our homes and feeding them when necessary.

Early Christians practiced hospitality in their missionary outreach. As God's servants left their homes

124

to spread the gospel in distant places they found the pagan world hostile and the inns exorbitant. Had it not been for hospitable brethren who took them into their homes, their ministries would have been greatly limited. And we are to be no less hospitable today than they were then.

Are you?

The fourth has to do with spiritual gifts. In verses 10 and 11 Peter writes, "As each one has received a special gift, employ it in serving one another, as good stewards of the manifold grace of God. Whoever speaks, let him speak, as it were, the utterances of God; whoever serves, let him do so as by the strength which God supplies: so that in all things God may be glorified through Jesus Christ to whom belongs the glory and dominion forever and ever. Amen."

Peter emphasizes three great truths concerning spiritual gifts: first, every Christian has been given at least one spiritual gift. Second, his spiritual gift is either a speaking gift such as preaching, teaching and witnessing—or a serving gift with which he ministers to human need on the physical level.

If he has a speaking gift, he is to use it to proclaim the utterances of God, *i.e.,* the truths of His word. If he has a serving gift, he is to avail himself of the strength that God supplies in using it to meet the needs of others. And third, the Christian is not to use his gift in self-glorification; instead he is to use it to bring honor to the name of our Lord Jesus Christ. And if he does just that, one day he will hear his Master say, "Well done, thou good and faithful servant."

Will you?

9

---

1 Peter 5:1-14

THE PASTOR'S TASK

Simon Peter makes it clear that the man who hears and heeds God's call to be a pastor will have his hands full, and without divine help he won't be able to make it.

In the New Testament there are three words that refer to the office of pastor: (1) *Presbuteros*—elder; this indicates the dignity of the office, for an elder is one worthy of respect; (2) *Episkopos*—bishop; this has to do with the work of a pastor as an overseer; and (3) *Poimenes*—pastor; this has to do with the shepherding responsibilities of the pastor.

Peter addresses his remarks to the elders (presbuterous), and then he commands that they shepherd the flock of God. The verb "to shepherd" is *poimaino,* the same word from which we get our English word "pastor." In using these two words he illustrates the fact that they refer to the same New Testament office: the pastor is to have the same relationship to the people entrusted to his care as a shepherd does to his flock. In calling this to his fellow pastors' attention, Peter was actually giving them four commandments, all of which are derived from the meaning of the verb "to shepherd." These are:

1. Feed the Flock of God—the pastor's responsibility as a preacher and a teacher.

2. Protect the Flock of God—the pastor's responsibility as a prophet.

3. Love the Flock of God—the pastor's responsibility as God's undershepherd in the church.

4. Lead the Flock of God—the pastor's responsibility as an administrator.

Feed the Flock of God. Peter was personally given this command three times directly from the Lord Jesus Himself. (See John 21:15-17.)

From this experience there was no doubt in his mind that this is one of the prime responsibilities of the pastor. It is incumbent upon him as a preacher and a teacher to feed his flock upon the Word of God. These two concepts go hand in hand; they are inseparable. Each sermon that he preaches must have a teaching element in it, and each lesson that he teaches should have a challenge inherent within it.

Peter explains in the first verse of chapter 5 that he was a witness of the suffering of Christ. The word he uses for "witness" pictures one who is a spectator and eyewitness, one who testifies to what he has seen and is willing to suffer and die for that testimony. It comes from the same Greek word from which we get our English word "martyr." Peter was saying, "I really know the Saviour; I saw Him suffer agony on the cross. Since that time I have constantly borne witness to what He has done for me through His sufferings. The day will finally come when I shall gladly die for Him."

This is the quality of relationship every minister of the gospel must have if he is going to produce the maximum in his preaching and teaching ministry. Like Enoch of old, through a deep devotional life the effective preacher and teacher must daily walk with the Lord.

A pastor must have a thorough knowledge of the Word of God. It is incumbent upon him that he be able to divide rightly the Word of Truth. While in seminary he is given the tools with which to do this. It is imperative that he spend long hours in study every week. Under the guidance of the Holy Spirit he must literally saturate himself with deep scriptural truth. Only after doing this is he really prepared to be God's messenger from the pulpit.

Protect the Flock of God. This command is pertinent to the pastor as a prophet. Just as the Great Shepherd of the sheep protects His flock eternally, so it is the responsibility of the undershepherd, the pastor, to protect his flock from false teachers who seek to destroy them intellectually and spiritually.

God holds pastors accountable for being informed about false doctrines which are prevalent and for warning their people against them. In our day this includes the Jehovah's Witnesses, the Mormons, the Christian Scientists, "situational ethics," the occult, and an ever-increasing drug culture.

131

Let me give you a case in point. Many people in our churches today are hung up on astrology. The first thing they read each morning is their astrological chart; and many will not make a major decision without consulting it. A pastor, interested in protecting his flock, must cry out against this, pointing out to his people that the Bible teaches that astrology is of the devil and comes under the condemnation of God Himself.

Love the Flock of God. This has to do with the pastor as God's undershepherd in the church. Scripture reveals that the shepherd has a profound love for each of the sheep in his flock. The parable of Jesus recorded in Luke 15:3-7 readily comes to mind.

After the sheep were in the fold and had been counted that night, the shepherd discovered that one was missing. Somewhere out in the darkness one was lost. Motivated by love, he went out in search of that lamb. When he found him, he rejoiced and summoned his neighbors to a party saying, "Rejoice with me, for I have found my sheep which was lost!" (v. 6).

Like that shepherd, the pastor must love every member of his church, even those whom he finds difficult to like. A man may be a profound biblical scholar, a peerless pulpiteer, and a modern Jeremiah when it comes to warning his church members concerning the dangers confronting them. But if he doesn't love his people, it will not be long until his ministry will begin to disintegrate and lose its effectiveness.

Lead the Flock of God. This has to do with the pastor as an administrator. Notice that the command stipulates that the pastor is to lead—not drive the

132

flock of God. It is most significant that the Bible calls Christians sheep and not cattle. The analogy is clear. Sheep are to be led; cattle are to be driven.

The pastor is not to lord it over his people, but he is to be their example. As an administrator he must keep himself above reproach by putting into practice what he preaches. It is mandatory that he be able to say to his people as Paul wrote to the Corinthians, "Be imitators of me, just as I also am of Christ" (1 Cor. 11:1).

In 1 Thessalonians 5:22 Paul tells us that every Christian is to abstain from all appearance of evil. This is especially true of a pastor. Indiscretion on his part can be as devastating as immorality.

In verse 4 we are told that when the Chief Shepherd appears, the pastor who has been faithful in feeding, protecting, loving and leading his flock will receive the unfading crown of glory. I do not know what that crown is; the Bible doesn't say. But I am sure that if the Lord has prepared it for His faithful pastors, it is of infinite value.

EVERYONE'S TASK

We discover in First Peter that the Big Fisherman faced problems similar to ones pastors face today. People are in trouble and crying for help. Confusion and upheaval bring problems into their lives which simply overwhelm them. Fortunately both for Peter and for us, God gave him an answer. "You younger men, likewise, be subject to your elders; and all of you, clothe yourselves with humility toward one another, for God is opposed to the proud, but gives grace to the humble. Humble yourselves, therefore, under the mighty hand of God, that He may exalt you at the proper time, casting all your anxiety upon Him, because He cares for you" (1 Pet. 5:5-7).

The person who applies Simon Peter's therapy, which in reality is God's therapy, discovers that it works. It pulls him out of the doldrums, puts a spring in his step, a song in his heart, and makes life really worth living.

An act of the mind is involved in which four basic facts of life are recognized. In the first place, you and I cannot solve our problem by ourselves. We must have the help of our fellow man and almighty God. This is the point of verse 5 and the first part of verse 6. Young men are to relate themselves properly to those who are older, for they need their help in solving the problems of life. All of us are to clothe ourselves with humility, recognizing that by so doing we shall have God's assistance in solving the problems which are too difficult for us to handle.

In the second place, God really cares about us. Christianity is different from every other religion because the story of other religions is the story of man seeking God; but the story of Christianity is the story of God seeking man who is the object of His compassionate love. John, in describing Jesus, said, "Having loved His own which were in the world, He loved them to the end" (John 13:1). David wrote, "I cried unto God with my voice, even unto God with my voice"† (notice he repeats this to make sure the reader gets it); "and he gave ear unto me" (Ps. 77:1). If you are going to find a solution to problems that seem to be wiping you out, you must realize that you can have the same experience as David.

You can cry unto God, and He will give ear unto you because He cares about you.

In the third place, God is able to meet our needs. Notice the first part of verse 6, "Humble yourselves, therefore, under the mighty hand of God." This Old Testament expression is used many times in connection with God delivering His people from Egyptian slavery and ushering them into the promised land. "The Lord your God brought you out of there by a mighty hand and by an outstretched arm." (See Deut. 26:8.) With that same mighty hand which is always extended to us, God can meet your need and mine. Paul realized this and said, "I can do all things through Him who strengthens me" (Phil. 4:13). For through the Son, God the Father extends His mighty hand to us.

Finally, remember God works on His own time schedule. In verse 6 Simon Peter informs us that, if we will implement his suggestions, God will give us the solution to our problems. But this He will do on the basis of His time schedule, not ours. We always want things done yesterday, but this isn't the way He works. Notice Peter says ". . . that He may exalt you at the proper time."

In solving problems which frustrate us and threaten to destroy us, not only is an act of the mind imperative, but also an act of the will. The Big Fisherman points out that this act is both an act of humility and an act of transference.

Peter writes, "Humble yourselves, therefore, under the mighty hand of God." The action of our Lord Jesus Christ in the garden of Gethsemane is a perfect example of what is involved in this. Three times He

135

prayed that the cup be removed from Him; but each time He added, "Nevertheless not My will, but Thine be done." Jesus humbled Himself under the mighty hand of His Father. The Lord Jesus demonstrated to us humility when He prayed, "Not My will, but Thine be done," and then He carried out the will of the Father.

We will not begin to solve the problems that frustrate us until we are willing to pray, "Not My will, but Thine be done," and then act in concert with that will when God reveals it. This is the point at which true humility is achieved. Peter points out in the last part of verse 5 that God is opposed to the proud but gives grace to the humble.

The second act of the will is one of transference. Peter wrote, "casting all your anxiety upon Him, because He cares for you" (v. 7). Notice the word "all." We are to transfer all of our anxieties, all of our difficulties, all of our frustrations to the Lord Jesus Christ. As long as we harbor any of these things within us, they are going to continue to frustrate us.

THE DEVIL'S WORK

"The devil will get you if you don't watch out," is a cliche that parents have used through the years to get their children to do what they want them to do. In spite of the fact that it has been misused in this way, this phrase is a very good paraphrase of 1 Peter 5:8, "Be of sober spirit, be on the alert. Your adversary, the devil, prowls about like a roaring lion, seeking someone to devour." Peter goes on, "But resist him, firm in your faith, knowing that the same experiences of suffering are being accomplished by your brethren who are in the world. And after you have suffered for a little, the God of all grace, who called you to His eternal glory in Christ, will Himself perfect, confirm, strengthen and establish you." In these three verses seven facts are called to our attention and four important commands are issued to every believer.

First of all, Peter points out that the devil is a living personality. This he does by the use of the pronouns in referring to him. Look once again at verse 8 and the first part of verse 9. Here he refers to the devil as "he" and as "whom," not as "it" and "which." From experience the Big Fisherman knew him to be a living personality. Many times he had met him on the field of combat and suffered defeat at his hands. There came that time during the trial of the Lord Jesus when Peter was given an opportunity to take a stand for Jesus Christ. But instead of taking that stand he listened to the devil and denied the Lord—not once, but three times, and the third time he used profanity and blasphemy to back up his denial.

Through the years there have been and there are today people who try to eliminate the idea of a personal devil. The Bible says that the devil is a person. And be assured that anyone who tries to live his life for Jesus Christ day by day will soon realize this fact because he will meet him face to face.

The evangelist, Bud Robinson, tells of a man who boldly stated, "I don't believe in a personal devil because I have never met him." Bud Robinson answered, "You never will meet him because you are walking in the same direction he is. It is only when

137

you are going in an opposite direction that you meet anyone."

Second, Simon Peter points out that the devil is the master of camouflage. Here he speaks of him as a roaring lion. In the book of Genesis he is presented as a serpent; in the Gospel of Matthew, in the temptation of our Lord, he is pictured as the Prince of the Power of the air. Paul tells us in 2 Corinthians 11:14 that Satan can transform himself into an angel of light. Yes, he is the master of camouflage and as such he presents himself as a most attractive individual.

Third, he also makes his program exceedingly attractive to people. We are human beings with sensual desires and when those sensual desires are fulfilled, it is enticing and attractive. But don't be fooled by his camouflage. The person who follows what he has to offer is ultimately defeated and doomed.

Fourth, Peter reveals to us that the devil is the enemy of righteousness. He speaks of the devil as his adversary and the word adversary comes from two Greek words, *anti* meaning "against" and *dikos* meaning "righteousness." The devil is against every form of righteousness that is known to man. He is against God at every turn.

In practically every religious course which is taught in the secular university the professor takes the position that God is the Father of all men and therefore all men are brothers; therefore, we have universal salvation. I want you to look at John 8:44. Jesus says, "You are of your father the devil." If the devil is the father of some, then God can't be the Father of all.

Jesus goes on to say, "He was a murderer from the beginning, and does not stand in the truth, because there is no truth in him. Whenever he speaks a lie, he speaks from his own nature; for he is a liar, and the father of lies."

Fifth, Peter informs us that the devil is extremely active. He is the personification of perpetual motion. The devil is always walking about and is always seeking; he never stops. We are told concerning the Lord Jesus Christ that He neither slumbers nor sleeps, and the same thing is true of the devil. He is always active.

Sixth, the devil is no respecter of persons. He is after the rich and the poor, the educated and the uneducated, the cultured and the uncultured, the religious and the nonreligious; all are alike to him. Dedicated Christians get the impression that because they love the Lord everything is going to be all right as far as their homes are concerned. Don't you believe this. The devil is after the Christian home more than he is any other type. I had lunch with a fine Christian educator, and one of the most effective pulpiteers in the United States. He, along with his wife, has given his life to serving Jesus Christ. He told me with tears in his eyes, "My oldest daughter is divorced; my second daughter is married to a drunk and is on her way to a divorce; my boy came home with some college friends, boys and girls, and they insisted on sleeping together in my home, and I had to throw them out." The devil is no respecter of persons. All Christian parents should be alert and do all within their power to help their children understand the techniques of the devil so that they can withstand him.

Seventh, the devil's purpose is always destructive. We are told in verse 8 that he is seeking anyone he may devour. "Devour" is a picture word that can be used to portray a little boy coming in after school, so hungry he can hardly stand it. He finds a glass of milk and three or four cookies on the table and quick as you can wink your eye he devours all the food. This is what the devil wants to do with each and every one of us. His desire is to devour us.

Now, notice the four commands. Three of them are stated directly and the fourth is implied. Peter commands in verse 8, "Be sober," which can also be translated "be sane." Satan is constantly after the Christians of every generation to disregard this command. For Christians to yield to Satan would lead to their undoing and the complete destruction of their testimony. It would be spiritual insanity. Hence he commands, "be sane" or "don't let the devil pull the wool over your eyes either as to who he is or what his purposes are. I have given you the straight story."

Then Peter commands, "Be on the alert" (v. 8) or "be ever watching." Those who do not heed this command soon find themselves in trouble. A young man I know said, "When I came home from Viet Nam, I thought I had to drink in order to relax. I really went to sleep as to what the devil was doing to me. I started with beer, got on the hard stuff and started playing poker. I am just miserable. I know that if I don't call it quits now I'm ruined. Why, oh, why did I go to sleep when I should have been awake?"

The third command is found in verse 9, "Resist him, firm in your faith." The weapons of our resistance are prayer, Bible study, and Christian service. In James 4:7 we are told that if we resist him in this way he will flee from us.

Simon Peter implies that we are to recognize that by carrying out these other three commands, ultimately we are going to gain the victory over all the forces of evil that Satan can muster. In *The Living Bible* this verse is translated, "After you have suffered a little while, our God, who is full of kindness through Christ, will give you his eternal glory. He personally will come and pick you up, and set you firmly in place, and make you stronger than ever" (1 Pet. 5:10). What a graphic description of the rapture this is. We may suffer now. We may be under constant attack from the devil now; but this will not always be so. When He comes for His own, the victory will be ours.

THE FINALE

In the finale of his first epistle, the Big Fisherman writes, "To Him be dominion forever and ever. Amen. Through Silvanus, our faithful brother (for so I regard him), I have written to you briefly, exhorting and testifying that this is the true grace of God. Stand firm in it! She who is in Babylon, chosen together with you, sends you greetings, and so does my son, Mark. Greet one another with a kiss of love. Peace be to you all who are in Christ" (1 Pet. 5:11-14).

Reversing the order, let us consider verses 12-14 first. Some critics claim that Peter couldn't possibly have written this epistle. The Holy Spirit answers this criticism in verse 12 by pointing out that Silvanus, a Roman citizen also known as Silas, worked with Peter in putting the epistle into such beautiful literary form. This verse also calls our attention to the fact that the true grace of God is revealed in the epistle and that you and I as Christians are to stand firm in it. We are to let the world know, both by what we say and by what we do, that we are staking our eternal destinies on the truths which the epistle delineates.

There are two schools of thought as to the identity of the "she" who sends greetings in verse 13, the Babylon from which the greetings are sent, and the Mark who shares in the greetings. Let us examine each of these.

In the first place there are those who believe that the "she" refers to the wife of Simon Peter. There is no doubt but that she was active in serving Christ, accompanying her husband on his preaching missions and assisting him. First Corinthians 9:5 makes this clear: "Do we not have a right to take along a believing wife, even as the rest of the apostles, and the brothers of the Lord, and Cephas?"

On the other hand there are those who believe that the "she" refers to a church located in the city Peter calls Babylon. Some feel Babylon refers to the ancient city of Babylon where the Jews were exiled following the fall of Judah. Many of them remained in that land even when they were given a chance to return home. There was a thriving Jewish community there during the New Testament era. It is conceivable that Peter could have gone there, ministered to the people, and established a church. Both John Calvin and Erasmus were convinced that he did. This is unlikely, however, since there is no other reference in literature to his ever visiting that city.

Most likely Babylon refers to Rome, which is actually called by that name in Revelation 17 and 18. There is no doubt but that the godlessness, the lust, and the sensuous luxury of ancient Babylon were reincarnate in Rome during the time of the New Testament.

Scholars also disagree as to the identity of Mark. There are those who are convinced that Mark was the son of Peter and his wife, and that he traveled with them on their missionary outreaches for Christ. However, the Mark mentioned here is more likely the same one who wrote the Gospel of Mark. William Barclay spells this out, "Papias, who lived towards the end of the second century, and who was a great collector of early traditions, describes Mark's Gospel in this way: 'Mark, who was Peter's interpreter, wrote down accurately though not in order, all that he recollected of what Christ had said or done. For he was not a hearer of the Lord or a follower of His; he followed Peter'. . . . According to Papias, Mark's Gospel is nothing other than the preaching material of Peter. . . . It is the consistent story of tradition that Mark was indeed a son to Peter, and all the likelihood is that the greetings are from him."[1]

Verse 14 calls to our attention a custom in the early church. Peter expresses it, "Greet one another with a kiss of love. Peace be to you all who are in Christ." In the early days the kiss was an important part of the communion service. It was usually given after the nonmembers of the church had been dismissed. Before partaking of the elements the members would kiss each other, symbolizing the fact that they loved one another and were at peace. It was a beautiful, meaningful and worshipful experience for them. As time went on it became merely a ritual, completely losing its true significance. Eventually the practice stopped altogether.

The message for the modern church in verse 14 is that God expects her membership to love and to live at peace with one another. Where this spirit prevails people are drawn to Jesus Christ as their Saviour and Lord, and the church grows.

Have you ever wondered why Christians suffer? In verses 10 and 11 Peter gives two answers. He writes, "And after you have suffered for a little, the God of all grace, who called you to His eternal glory in Christ, will Himself perfect, confirm, strengthen and establish you. To Him be dominion forever and ever. Amen."

Why do Christians suffer? The first reason is that through suffering God perfects them for His service. In the Greek language there are two words for the verb, "to perfect." The first and most common is *teleioo,* which means "to perfect in the sense of bringing to maturity and completion." This is not the word used here.

The second is *katartizo* which means "to repair, to fit together, to supply, to make good, to restore to a useful condition, to reinstate." W. E. Vine in his *Expository Dictionary of New Testament Words* points out that it means "to render fit."[2] The basic idea is that of putting parts in a right relationship and connection one with another. Kenneth Wuest illuminates the meaning of the word as he writes, "It is the same word translated 'perfecting' in Ephesians 4:12, where the gifted servants of the Lord

144

mentioned were given to the church for the equipping of the saints for ministering work. The word was used of James and John mending their nets, thus equipping them for service (Mark 1:19). Here the word refers to God mending the lives of Christians, thus equipping them for usefulness in His service. The word in First Peter speaks of the work of the Holy Spirit in rounding out the spiritual life of the saint so that he is equipped for both the living of a Christian life and the service of the Lord Jesus."[3]

One of the prime reasons God allows Christians to suffer is that they might be perfected through that suffering for effective Christian service. Experience bears testimony to the fact that this really works.

The late George W. Truett is a case in point. While hunting one day with one of his closest friends, he accidentally shot and killed him. This resulted in his suffering untold agony both spiritually and emotionally as he constantly brooded over what had happened. Finally he knelt and prayed, "Father, if You will give me the strength for the rest of my life I will do the work of two men in serving Christ." And he did. Even though he went to be with the Lord in the early 1940s, his influence for good continues to be felt today. The Holy Spirit mended the broken net of his heart, perfected him through suffering, and used him to reach the masses for the Saviour.

Yes, God allows Christians to suffer in order that they may be perfected in their service for the Saviour. We who love the Lord should have the same attitude as Paul had when he wrote in Romans 5:3-5, "And not only this, but we also exult in our tribulations, knowing that tribulation brings about perseverance;

145

and perseverance, proven character; and proven character, hope; and hope does not disappoint, because the love of God has been poured out within our hearts through the Holy Spirit who was given to us."

Three words are used in 1 Peter 5:10 to describe the second reason God allows Christians to suffer—confirm, strengthen and establish. "Confirm" comes from the verb *sterixo* which means "to settle, to confirm, to ground as on a foundation." "Strengthen" is derived from *sthenoo* which literally means "to strengthen, or to impart strength." And "establish" comes from *themelioo* which means "to establish on a foundation." When these three words are taken together, they convey the idea that God allows Christians to suffer in order that their faith may be strengthened so that nothing can separate them from the eternal foundation which God Himself has laid—Jesus Christ.

In commenting on this William Barclay wrote, "Suffering of body and sorrow of heart do one of two things to a man. They either make him collapse; or, out of them, he comes with a solidarity of character which he could never have gained anywhere else."[4]

John, the beloved, is a good example. Through the suffering which he experienced as an old man exiled to the Isle of Patmos, his faith was greatly strengthened. And as the result the Spirit of God used him to write the book of Revelation.

A man who belongs to the church where I am now serving has really experienced a testing of his faith. Several years ago he was operated on for brain cancer. When the doctor got on the inside, he discovered

146

that he could not remove the tumor. He simply froze it and sewed the man up. The man reacted to that adversity by dedicating his life to serve the Lord through his chosen profession. God has prospered him for this, and his faith through it all has been like the Rock of Gibraltar.

Then he had a massive heart attack. Can you imagine what his first words to me were? "Preacher, I am right with the Lord. It doesn't make any difference whether He takes me home or leaves me here. I am going to serve Him. Please tell everyone that this is a great feeling." And by this he meant a tremendous assurance. Once again his faith was put to the test and once again his faith was strengthened by it. He is well on his way now to complete recovery, and he can hardly wait to resume his church responsibilities which are both heavy and significant.

With his life this man is saying what Peter wrote in verse 11, "To Him be dominion for ever and ever. Amen."

What are you saying with yours?

Footnotes
1. Barclay, *The Letters of James and Peter,* p. 330.
2. Vine, *Expository Dictionary of New Testament Words,* p. 175.
3. Wuest, *First Peter in the Greek New Testament,* p. 131.
4. Barclay, *The Letters of James and Peter,* p. 324.

Second Peter

10

---

2 Peter 1:1-11

BASIC TO THE FAITH

In all probability the most neglected book in the entire New Testament is Second Peter. It was not admitted into the New Testament until the last part of the fourth century A.D. Nevertheless, it has a message of great spiritual import, a message that you and I can study with great profit. For you see it speaks to us right at the point where we live day by day. "Basic to the faith" and "down to earth" are phrases that characterize its content.

We begin our study by looking at verse 1 of the third chapter. There Peter writes, "This is now, beloved the second letter I am writing to you in which I am stirring up your sincere mind by way of reminder." First and Second Peter were both addressed to the same group of Christians who were suffering for their faith.

Bondslaves

Peter writes in 1:1, "Simon Peter, a bond-servant and apostle of Jesus Christ, to those who have received a faith of the same kind as ours, by the righteousness of our God and Saviour, Jesus Christ." In this verse we are brought face to face with three important truths. First we are confronted by inference with the truth that every Christian basically is a bond servant of Jesus Christ. As believers we are not privileged characters. We are slaves; this is the precise meaning of the Greek *doulos* which is used. Look carefully at that first verse and you will notice a significant thing about the sequence of it. He mentions that he is a bond servant before he calls attention to his apostleship. Peter recognized that above and beyond everything else, he was a slave of the Saviour.

All the great biblical saints are pictured in this way. In Psalm 105:26 we read, "He sent Moses His servant." Here the Psalmist calls Moses a bondslave of God.

If you were to ask a Jew today to tell you who was the greatest king in the history of Israel, his response would be, "David." In Psalm 119:125 this man among men writes concerning his relationship to his Maker, "I am Thy servant." Despite the fact that he was an absolute monarch, first and foremost, he was a bondslave.

The most productive Christian that ever lived was the apostle Paul. The greatest book that he wrote from the standpoint of its theological content is the book of Romans. It is quite significant to note the way in which he begins this theological treatise. He writes, "Paul, a bond-servant of Christ Jesus, called as an apostle." Like Peter, Paul points out the fact that he was a bondslave before he mentions his apostleship. My friends, it doesn't make any difference what height we achieve in Christianity, what greatness comes our way, we are all like Moses, David, Paul and Peter, we are bondslaves of the Lord Jesus Christ.

Because we are bondslaves God owns us. He possesses us. One of the ways in which a man became a bondslave in ancient days was to be purchased out of the slave market by his master. What a picture that is of what Christ has done for us. Each and every one of us was in the slave market of sin, and our Lord Jesus Christ purchased our redemption and made us new creations in Himself.

In 1 Corinthians 6:19, Paul writes, "Or do you not know that your body is a temple of the Holy Spirit who is in you, whom you have from God, and that you are not your own?" Don't you dare get up and say, "I am the master of my fate. I am the master of my own life. I am the master of my own time." If you are a Christian, you are not your own. Why not? Because, "you have been bought with a price: therefore glorify God in your body" (v. 20). The price that God paid for your redemption and mine is the shed blood of the Master on Calvary's cross.

Because we are bondslaves, Christ has the right to expect complete obedience from us. In ancient days a slave did what his master said. So it is with our relationship to our Lord Jesus Christ. We should only be asking one question, "What will You have me to do, Lord?"

Because we are bondslaves, the Lord Jesus Christ has the right to expect continual service out of us. "In the ancient world the slave had no holidays, no working hours settled by agreement, no leisure. All his time belonged to the master."[1] So it is with those of us who are Christians. As bondslaves we have no right to compartmentalize our lives. All of our time, talent and treasury belong to our Master. Unfortunately, most Christians do not have this concept of themselves. They compartmentalize their lives, relegating Christ to one hour a week when it is convenient. When it is not convenient, they simply forget it.

Nevertheless, in spite of our shortcomings and our failures, God deals with us in love, forgiveness, and mercy. He is always ready to take us back and restore us to fellowship.

Equal Before God

Peter calls attention to the fact that every Christian's faith is of equal value in God's sight. Notice the way he puts it in the last part of verse 1, "to those who have received a faith of the same kind as ours, by the righteousness of our God and Saviour, Jesus Christ." Look at the phrase, "of the same kind." This is a translation of *isotimon* which is made up of two Greek words, *iso* meaning "equal" and *timon* meaning "honor, value and privilege." Every Christian before the Lord is equal as far as his faith is concerned in value, honor and privilege. He says here that we have received this faith that makes us equal. The word "to receive" is *lachousin,* better translated "allotted" or "given." We have been allotted or given this faith by God Himself. The word "faith" is used here as a synonym for salvation. Notice the words, "By the righteousness of our God and Saviour, Jesus Christ." It is by the righteousness of our God and Saviour Jesus Christ that you and I have been given this salvation that makes us equal before God in privilege, in value and in honor.

In 2 Peter 1:1 we read, "To those who have received a faith of the same kind as ours." To whom does "ours" refer? The answer—Peter, James, John, and the other apostles. Just think, when you and I accept Jesus Christ as Saviour, the salvation allotted to us makes us equal before God in value, honor and privilege to the apostles like Peter, James, John and Paul. Did you ever think you were as important to God as they are? You are. You see, God doesn't recognize any hierarchy; there are no privileged characters in His sight. We are all equal before Him.

Grace and Peace

"Grace and peace be multiplied to you in the knowledge of God and Jesus our Lord" (2 Pet. 1:2). Even though this is a brief prayer which Peter offers in behalf of his persecuted friends, spiritual truth of infinite value oozes out of every facet of it. It consists of two parts: first, the prayer itself; and second, the means by which God will answer it.

Seven words constitute the prayer, "Grace and peace be multiplied to you." God offers to each of us peace with Himself. Paul points this out in Romans 5:1, "Therefore having been justified by faith, we have peace with God through our Lord Jesus Christ." God in grace—which is the Almighty thinking in terms of what man needs rather than what he deserves—sent

His only begotten Son, Jesus Christ, to die on Calvary to pay the penalty of our wrongdoing. When we by faith invite Him into our lives as Saviour and Lord, He accepts the invitation. He comes in. He establishes peace between us and our heavenly Father. This peace with God is a permanent possession; it can never be taken from us.

The Almighty also offers to us the peace of God. This is that peace which gives us a sense of satisfaction and a warm inner feeling of contentment. It comes to us as a result of our allowing the Holy Spirit to control our lives completely. If we refuse to do this, this peace, unlike "peace with God," can be and will be taken from us. Paul writes about this peace in Philippians 4:6,7, "Be anxious for nothing, but in everything by prayer and supplication with thanksgiving let your requests be made known to God. And the peace of God, which surpasses all comprehension, shall guard your hearts and minds in Christ Jesus." Here he points out that the secret of having this peace of God in our lives is twofold. First, we must be free from anxiety; second, we must have a proper prayer life. Both of these are impossible apart from the controlling of the Holy Spirit in our lives.

I know some very frustrated, unhappy, discontented and disgruntled Christians. They do not have the peace of God in their lives and the reason for this is very elementary. Even though they have accepted Christ as Saviour, they insist on being the masters of their own lives. They shun the directives of the Holy Spirit and consequently grieve Him—which Christians are commanded not to do. Paul spells this out specifically, "And do not grieve the Holy Spirit of God, by whom you were sealed for the day of redemption" (Eph. 4:30).

If you are in this situation, our heavenly Father still makes available to you the peace of God. Simply let His Spirit take charge of your life. Darkness will turn to light, sorrow to joy, unhappiness to happiness, frustration to contentment, dissatisfaction to satisfaction, and you will really begin to live. You will be able to heed Paul's admonition, "Rejoice in the Lord always; again I will say, rejoice!" (Phil. 4:4).

God Will Answer

As we think about all of this, we can understand why Peter prayed for his persecuted Christian friends whom he loved, "Grace and peace be multiplied to you." But not only does he pray this for them, he informs them how they can be assured God will answer this prayer in the affirmative, "in the knowledge of God and Jesus our Lord."

The key word in this phrase is "knowledge." It comes from the Greek word *epignosis* which has a threefold significance: According to J. Armitage Robinson *epignosis* is knowledge that is directed toward a particular object.[2] In this verse Peter by inference is pointing out that grace and peace will be multiplied in the life of the believer whose knowledge is directed toward Jesus Christ. This is just another way of saying that the more you and I know of Christ, the more we will understand the meaning of grace and the significance of peace, and the greater our experience will be of both.

In the light of this the question naturally arises, "How can I increase my knowledge of the Saviour?"

159

Let's let Jesus answer this question for us. In John 5 we find Him speaking to His enemies who were bent on killing Him because He had healed a man on the Sabbath. In defending Himself he said in verse 39, "You search the Scriptures, because you think that in them you have eternal life; and it is these that bear witness of Me." The more we get into the Word of God, the greater is our knowledge of Jesus Christ and our relationship to Him.

Epignosis means full knowledge. William Barclay in commenting on this points out that Plutarch "uses it of the scientific knowledge of music as opposed to the knowledge of the mere amateur. So it may be that the implication here is that knowledge of Jesus Christ is what we might call 'the master-science of life.' The other sciences may bring new skill, new knowledge, new abilities, but the master-science, the knowledge of Jesus Christ, alone brings the grace men need and the peace for which their hearts crave."[3]

Epignosis is knowledge that unites the subject with the object. This is what happens to a person when by faith he comes to know Jesus Christ as his Saviour and Lord. This knowledge actually unites him with the Master, with the result that grace and peace are multiplied to him. The apostle Paul expressed it this way in Galatians 2:20, "I have been crucified with Christ; and it is no longer I who live, but Christ lives in me; and the life which I now live in the flesh I live by faith in the Son of God, who loved me, and delivered Himself up for me."

Are grace and peace being multiplied in your life? How well do you really know Jesus Christ?

JESUS IS GOD

Next Peter makes it clear that Jesus Christ is God. He writes, "Our God and Saviour, Jesus Christ," and he tells us what kind of God Jesus is by pointing out seven truths concerning Him.

He points out that Jesus Christ is the *God of power*. The word "power" comes from the Greek *dunamis* from which we get our English words "dynamite" and "dynamic." Christ, the God of power, has the spiritual dynamite to explode sin from the life of a person, and the dynamic to make his life worth living.

Peter calls to our attention that Jesus is the *generous God*. He writes, "His divine power has granted to us everything pertaining to life and godliness, through the true knowledge of Him." The word translated "granted" is from *doreomai* which literally means "freely given." It is in the perfect passive tense which indicates that, once the gift has been given, it is ever the individual's possession.

Peter refers to Jesus as the *God of glory*. He writes, "Who called us by His own glory." The Beloved Apostle in writing about this aspect of our Lord said in John 1:14, "And the Word became flesh, and dwelt among us, and we beheld His glory, glory as the only begotten from the Father, full of grace and truth." On the Mount of Transfiguration Peter, James and John saw Christ glorified before them. You and I who are Christians are going to see Him that way at the rapture. Listen to the way John describes the glorious Christ: "And in the middle of the lampstands one like a son of man, clothed in a robe reaching to the feet, and girded across His breast with a golden

161

girdle. And His head and His hair were white like white wool, like snow; and His eyes were like a flame of fire; and His feet were like burnished bronze, when it has been caused to glow in a furnace, and His voice was like the sound of many waters. And in His right hand He held seven stars; and out of His mouth came a sharp two-edged sword; and His face was like the sun shining in its strength" (Rev. 1:13-16).

Peter tells us that Jesus is the *God of excellence.* The Greek word for excellence is *aretes.* It means "virtue" and "uprightness." Jesus is a God of virtue and uprightness. In Him there is no sin. I love the way *The Living Bible* presents this truth in 1 Peter 2:22,23, "He never sinned, never told a lie, never answered back when insulted; when he suffered he did not threaten to get even." And you and I must not overlook 2 Peter 2:21 where we are told that we are to follow in His steps. How are we doing?

Peter informs us that Jesus is the *God of promises.* In verse 4 we read, "For by these He has granted to us His precious and magnificent promises." The word for precious actually means "valuable" and the word for magnificent can be translated "extraordinarily wonderful." And that is exactly what His promises are. They are valuable and extraordinarily wonderful. Take for example the promise of 1 Thessalonians 4:13-18 that Christians are going to experience an eternal reunion. Down through the years this promise has enabled believers to stand the sorrow of death.

Peter calls to our attention that Jesus is the *God who makes every believer a sharer* in the divine nature. We read in verse 4, "in order that by them

you might become partakers of the divine nature."
The specific promise that applies to this truth is the
one Jesus made to Nicodemus in John 3:1-16. Jesus
promised him that if he would accept Him as Saviour
and Lord by faith, he would experience the new birth.
When you and I by faith turn ourselves over to Jesus
Christ we are born into God's family.

Peter asserts that Jesus is the *God who delivers*
the believer from the corruption that is in the world
by lust. He states in verse 4, "having escaped the
corruption that is in the world by lust." You and
I by nature have a bent toward sinning. However,
when we surrender ourselves to Christ, He enables
us to overcome the temptations which lead to
corruption.

ADD TO FAITH

In the first part of verse 5 we then find a connecting
statement joining the sevenfold description of Jesus
Christ as God with that which follows. Peter writes,
"Now for this very reason also, applying all diligence,
in your faith supply. . . ." And then he goes on to
tell us what we are to supply or add to our faith.
You shouldn't be content to be just a babe in Christ.
Christian growth and maturity are most desir-
able.

It is by faith that you and I are born into the family
of God. But our Christianity should not stop here.
Someone asked, "Isn't faith the end of the gospel?"
The reply came back, "Yes, the front end!" After
we have taken this step of faith, we are to begin
growing in that faith. We are to become adults for
Christ. In verses 5 through 7 Peter outlines seven

virtues that we are to add. Without these we cannot grow. With these we can become the mature persons our Saviour wants us to be. Let us carefully examine them.

Moral Excellence

First of all we are to add moral excellence. The word that is translated here is *aretes*. This is the same word used in verse 3 to describe Jesus Christ as the God of excellence, uprightness and virtue. It also means "courage," and this applies to us. If we are to mature in the Christian life we must be upright and virtuous, courageously taking our stand for that which is right regardless of the price we must pay. This means if you are a young lady and are desperately in love with a boy who tries to persuade you that this love allows him to be intimate with you, your answer is to be "no," even if it means breaking up with him. If you are a student and you have an opportunity to cheat on a test which will give you an A and put you in the honor society, you are to refuse to do so even if it means missing out on scholastic honors. If you are a businessman and have a chance to become involved in a shady deal which will give you enough money to save your business, you are to refuse to become involved even if you go broke. Mature Christians are those who are morally and ethically courageous, taking a stand for righteousness regardless of cost. Have you added this virtue to your faith?

Knowledge

To our moral excellence we are to add spiritual

knowledge. In Philippians 4:8 Paul wrote, "Finally, brethren, whatever is true, whatever is honorable, whatever is right, whatever is pure, whatever is lovely, whatever is of good repute, if there is any excellence and if anything worthy of praise, let your mind dwell on these things." As you and I saturate our minds with these things which are found only in the Scripture, we increase our spiritual knowledge and grow toward maturity.

A famous preacher of another generation admitted that the Bible was as dry as dust to him, and stated that this had to change or he would be forced by frustration to leave the ministry. He asked Dr. R. A. Torrey for advice.

"Read the Scripture," came the quick reply. "But I do read it," he complained. "Read it again," said Dr. Torrey. "Take some book and read it twelve times a day for a month." Then he suggested the preacher try Second Peter.

In telling about this the minister went on to say, "My wife and I read Second Peter three or four times in the morning, two or three times at noon, and three times at dinner. Soon I was speaking about Second Peter to everyone I met. It seemed as though the stars in the heavens were singing the story of Second Peter. I read Second Peter on my knees, marking passages. Teardrops mingled with the crayon colors, and I said to my wife, 'See how I have ruined my Bible.' 'Yes,' she said, 'but as the pages have been getting black, your life has been getting white.' " With the increase in biblical knowledge came the increase in spiritual growth. This is always the case. It is inevitable.

Self-Control

To our increase in biblical knowledge Peter commands that we add self-control. The Christian who gets mad and flies off the handle at the slightest provocation is a juvenile, and until he adds self-control he will continue to be a juvenile. The epitome of self-control is to be seen in Jesus Christ, who is not only our Saviour and Lord but also our example. While the two thieves, livid with anger, were cursing and crying out against their executioners, Jesus prayed, "Father, forgive them for they know not what they do." That is self-control raised to the superlative degree. You and I can do with a large amount of it.

Perseverance

To our self-control we are to add perseverance. This virtue has both a passive and an active aspect to it. The passive part is usually called patience. There are times when Christians are confronted with the necessity of making a major decision and the Lord's will is not immediately apparent. Instead of making the decision and then praying and asking God to bless it as most of us do, we should wait patiently for the Lord to reveal His will. This is hard to do, but nevertheless it is the right course of action. The Psalmist speaks, "Wait for the Lord; be strong, and let your heart take courage; yes, wait for the Lord" (Ps. 27:14). And the regal prophet echoes this same truth, "Yet those who wait for the Lord will gain new strength; they will mount up with wings like eagles, they will run and not get tired, they will walk and not become weary" (Isa. 40:31).

After we have waited for the Lord and He has

revealed His will, we are to persevere steadfastly in getting the job done. Jesus said in Luke 9:62, "No one, after putting his hand to the plough and looking back, is fit for the kingdom of God."

Jesus practiced what He preached. Isaiah 50:7 is a prophecy which quotes Him as saying, "Therefore, I have set My face like flint," and the inference is toward Calvary. He came into the world to die that men might live, and He let nothing deter Him from achieving His objective. The devil tried to dissuade Him by temptation, the general populace by seeking to make Him king, and His disciples by argument. But He turned a deaf ear to all. Resolutely He marched to the cross, experienced its pain until He said, "It is finished," and He gave up the ghost. He persevered until He completed His task which He came to do. This is what God expects us to do when He assigns us a task.

Godliness

To our perseverance we are to add godliness. The Greek word for this is *eusebeia* which has inherent within it two concepts: a right vertical relationship, and a right horizontal relationship; a right relationship with God and a right relationship with our fellow man. Are you in a right relationship to God and man? Do you realize that you have a duty to Him and to your fellow man? Are you carrying out those duties? If you are, you are on your way to maturity. If not, your spiritual growth is stunted.

Brotherly Kindness

We are to add to godliness brotherly kindness. The

word in the Greek is *philadelphia* which literally means "love of brother." As members of the body of Christ we as Christians are to love one another. We are to be sensitive to one another's needs. Paul tells us in 1 Corinthians 12:26 that we are to be so sensitive that if one member suffers we are all to suffer with him; suffer to the point of doing something about meeting his need. We are to be good Samaritans in our relationship to him.

Love

To brotherly kindness we are to add love. The word here is *agape,* and it means godly love. It goes beyond brotherly love and includes all outside of Christ.

In verses 8-11 Peter points out that the individual who has taken the step of faith in accepting Jesus Christ as Saviour has a choice to make between two alternatives. He can either refuse to add these virtues to his faith or by the power of the spirit he can strive to do so. If he makes the negative choice Peter tells us in verse 9 that he "is blind indeed, or at least very shortsighted, and has forgotten that God delivered him from the old life of sin so that now he can live a strong, good life for the Lord."†† And the tragedy of this is that most Christians have made this negative choice.

But notice what Peter says about those who make the positive choice. In verse 8 he teaches that they will truly grow in their knowledge, understanding and comprehension of the King of kings and Lord of lords; and they will produce Christian fruit with their lives.

In verse 10 Peter informs us that those who work

diligently at adding these seven spiritual virtues to their lives, give evidence that they have genuinely been called and chosen of God to be His children. There may be some doubt about those who don't do this, but there is none about those who do. Those who make the positive choice will not stumble. The word "stumble" comes from the Greek verb *ptaio* which also means "to fail." Those who engage in this heavenly addition will not fail in their Christian lives.

In verse 11 Peter calls to our attention that those who add to their faith moral excellence, and to their moral excellence knowledge, and to their knowledge self-control and to their self-control perseverance, and to their perseverance godliness, and to their godliness brotherly kindness, and to their brotherly kindness love, will receive a royal welcome into the kingdom of our Lord Jesus. The bands will be playing and the flags flying for them as they enter. *The Living Bible* puts it this way, "And God will open wide the gates of heaven for you to enter into the eternal kingdom of our Lord and Saviour Jesus Christ."

Are the gates going to be open for you in this way?

Footnotes
1. Barclay, *The Letters of James and Peter,* p. 346.
2. Vine, *Expository Dictionary of New Testament Words,* p. 299.
3. Barclay, *The Letters of James and Peter,* p. 348.

11

___

2 Peter 1:12-21

A PROMISE AND A PICTURE

"And I consider it right, as long as I am in this earthly dwelling, to stir you up by way of reminder, knowing that the laying aside of my earthly dwelling is imminent, as also our Lord Jesus Christ has made clear to me. And I will also be diligent that at any time after my departure you may be able to call these things to mind."

Promise

These verses center around a promise and a picture; a promise that Peter makes to the Christians of his day and a word picture which he paints of death. He states the promise in three ways: First, "Therefore, I shall always be ready to remind you of these things" (v. 12). A more accurate translation of this is,

"Wherefore I will not neglect to put you in remembrance always concerning these things." The verb "to put in remembrance" is the Greek word, *hupomimneskein* which is a present tense infinitive, indicating continuous action. The Big Fisherman was saying, "I am gently but everlastingly going to keep prodding you about your spiritual growth."

Second, Peter spells out the promise in this way, "And I consider it right, as long as I am in this earthly dwelling, to stir you up by way of reminder" (v. 13). The infinitive "to stir up" comes from the Greek verb *diegeiro*. It is a picture word which literally means "to stir up, to agitate" as an ocean gets stirred up and agitated in a great storm. Peter said, "I promise you that there will be times in my preaching when I am going to come on like a mighty wind. You will think that you have been hit by a typhoon. I am really going to get on your back about your failure to mature in the faith. I am going to clobber you."

Third, Peter writes, "And I will also be diligent that at any time after my departure you may be able to call these things to mind" (v. 15). And Peter did just this. Bible scholars generally accept that John Mark was a follower of Peter. Most of what he learned about Jesus was through Peter. Well-founded tradition has it that the Gospel of Mark is the preaching material of Peter.

As you and I think about these three ways in which Simon Peter stated this promise we need to recognize that he was pointing out the number one task of a pastor. It is his responsibility through his preaching and teaching ministry to consistently, gently prod his people about implementing the great truths of the Bible in their daily lives. He is never to let up on this.

Picture

Peter also in this section gives us a very graphic picture of what death for the Christian really is. In doing so he points out two important facts about his own death. He says in verse 14 that it is close at hand. He writes, "Knowing that the laying aside of my earthly dwelling is imminent." And second, in verse 14 by inference, he informs us that he would be executed. He states, "As also our Lord Jesus Christ has made clear to me." This statement takes us back to John 21:18,19. Following breakfast on the beach Jesus said to him, "Truly, truly, I say to you, when you were younger, you used to gird yourself, and walk wherever you wished; but when you grow old, you will stretch out your hands, and someone else will gird you, and bring you where you do not wish to go." John explains the meaning, "Now this He said, signifying by what kind of death he would glorify God" (v. 19). Peter was executed by crucifixion.

Although you and I do not know the manner in which we shall die, we can be assured that our death is imminent. Even though we may live another sixty to eighty years, this is only a drop in the bucket when measured against eternity. The Bible says in Hebrews 9:27, ". . . it is appointed for men to die once, and after this comes judgment." The sting of this experience can be greatly lessened or even removed for those who see the picture of death as Peter paints it for us.

He uses two words in his painting. The first is *apothesis* which literally means "a putting off," or "a laying aside." He speaks of death in verse 14 as "the laying aside of his earthly dwelling." When death occurs for the Christian he simply lays aside his physical body (that which holds him to the earth) and he goes to be with the Lord. Paul expresses this idea also in 2 Corinthians 5:8.

The second word Peter uses is *exodon* which literally means "exodus." As we turn back to the book of Exodus we discover that the exodus of the children of Israel was twofold: it was a departure, and it was an arrival. The children of Israel departed from Egypt and arrived in the promised land. This is what death for the Christian is. It is a departure from this life and an arrival into the eternal land of promise with the Lord Jesus.

As we put *apothesis* and *exodon* together we discover that Peter's picture of death for the believer is simply a laying aside of his physical body, a departure from this life and an arrival into the presence of the Saviour.

Death for the Christian is not a departing from this life to go out into an abyss of darkness and uncertainty. It is a departure from here to there, from earth to paradise, from an association with our friends and loved ones here to an eternal association with Jesus Christ and our Christian loved ones who have preceded us in death. And there is no defeat in this experience; it is completely triumphant. Paul wrote in 1 Corinthians 15:55-57, " 'O death, where is your victory? O death, where is your sting?' The sting of death is sin, and the power of sin is the law; but thanks be to God, who gives us the victory through our Lord Jesus Christ."

THE LORD'S SECOND COMING

Let us move on in our study to verses 16-18. "For we did not follow cleverly devised tales when we made known to you the power and coming of our Lord Jesus Christ, but we were eyewitnesses of His majesty. For when He received honor and glory from God the Father, such an utterance as this was made to Him by the Majestic Glory, 'This is My beloved Son with whom I am well pleased,'—and we ourselves heard this utterance made from heaven when we were with Him on the holy mountain."

As we study these verses we need to recognize that they were written during the time that his own death was very much in Simon Peter's mind. That which follows verse 15 is Peter's last will and testament for the Christians to whom he ministered. Even though he didn't have any material possessions to leave them, he did have some great truths which the Holy Spirit had revealed to him whereby their lives would be enriched spiritually. His was a burning desire to share these with them.

Verse 16 definitely refers to the second coming, not of the first coming of our Saviour. The word that is translated "coming" makes this crystal clear; it is the Greek *parousia* which is used throughout the New Testament to refer to our Lord's second advent. "The parousia is always a personal presence, never anything else. It is the King Himself—not even His kingdom—that we are to look for. . . . *Parousia* is traced in the East to the technical expression for the arrival

177

or the visit of the king or emperor. . . . It was in use in the time of the apostles, and they appropriated it for a sacred use. The coming, therefore, is the personal arrival."[1]

Jesus Himself used it: "For just as the lightning comes from the east, and flashes even to the west, so shall the coming (the parousia) of the Son of Man be" (Matt. 24:27); "For the coming (the parousia) of the Son of Man will be just like the days of Noah" (Matt. 24:37).

The doctrine of the second coming of Christ is not based on fiction but fact. It is not based upon the imagination but revelation. *The Living Bible* says in 2 Peter 1:16, "For we have not been telling you fairy tales when we explained to you the power of our Lord Jesus Christ and his coming again." Peter in his last will and testament makes it absolutely clear that his preaching of the second coming of Christ was not the figment of his imagination. It was fact. He believed the future well-being of the believer is dependent upon this coming event; it is his "blessed hope" (Titus 2:13).

In His first coming Jesus was the suffering, dying servant. In His second coming just the opposite will be true. Instead of being meek and lowly in heart He will come as the omnipotent King, smashing His enemies and establishing His universal kingdom. John, the beloved, gives a very accurate, descriptive picture of this in Revelation 19:11—20:3.

THE LORD'S KINGDOM IN MINIATURE

Peter relates the second coming of Christ and the establishing of His kingdom to his experience with the Lord on the Mount of Transfiguration. In order to understand the connection of this experience with the second coming of Christ and the establishing of His kingdom it is necessary for us to look at the Gospel accounts. It is found in Matthew 17:1-8; Mark 9:2-13; and Luke 9:28-36. Each of these records is preceded by a promise which the Lord gave to His disciples. Let us examine the Matthew record.

The prophetic promise is given, "Truly I say to you, there are some of those who are standing here who shall not taste death until they see the Son of Man coming in His kingdom" (Matt. 16:28). What did Jesus mean by this statement? The answer is found in the Mount of Transfiguration experience described in chapter 17, verses 1-8.

In this story the picture of our Lord's kingdom in miniature is given. There are four focal points that we need to examine carefully. The first is Jesus Himself. We are told in verse 2, "And He was transfigured before them; and His face shone like the sun, and His garments became as white as light." "Transfigured" comes from the Greek verb *metamorphoo* from which we get our English noun metamorphosis.

When Christ comes into His kingdom a metamorphosis will take place. Matthew tells us that His face will shine as the sun and His garments will become as white as lights (17:2). At that time He will be acknowledged by the people as the blessed and only Potentate, the King of kings and Lord of lords (see 1 Tim. 6:15).

The second focal point is Moses. Verse 3 informs us that he appeared on the Mount of Transfiguration and spoke with Jesus. As we zero in on Moses standing on the mount we see in him the representative of God's people who die before the rapture of the church and experience resurrection when that event occurs.

The third focal point is Elijah who is also described in verse 3 as conversing with the Saviour. Elijah represents the Christians who will be living at the time of the rapture. They will be transformed and translated to be with the Lord and will come back with Him when He establishes His kingdom.

Not only will these two groups be present when the Lord establishes His kingdom, but there will be another group made up of all who will be converted during the reign of the Antichrist. Our fourth focal point, that of Peter, James and John, is representative of this group. Like all human analogies of spiritual truth this one is incomplete. For in this fourth group there will be both Jews and Gentiles, and both those who survive the tribulation and those who experience martyrdom in it.

Yes, when Peter stood on the Mount of Transfiguration he saw in miniature the kingdom which our Lord will establish at His second coming. In writing about this experience Peter said, "We were eyewitnesses." The word "eyewitnesses" is the Greek *epoptes.* It was used in connection with the mystery religions of that day. When a person embraced one of these religions, he had to spend long hours in study before he finally reached the place where he was called an initiate. At that point he was permitted to be an *epoptes,* an "eyewitness" of a passion play in which he saw the suffering, the death and the resurrection of his god enacted on the stage.

180

Peter was an *epoptes* of the sufferings, the death and the resurrection of Jesus Christ. Through His experience on the Mount of Transfiguration he was also an *epoptes* of the glory and majesty of our Lord which will be His when He comes again and establishes His kingdom.

Not only was Peter an eyewitness to Christ's majesty and glory on the Mount of Transfiguration, he also heard the voice of God the Father saying, "This is my beloved Son, in whom I am well pleased; hear ye him"† (Matt. 17:5). This is the message we should heed right now. If we are Christians we need to hear our Saviour saying, "If you love Me, you will keep My commandments" (John 14:15). So many Christians fail Him at this point. They are willing to make Him their Saviour but not their Lord. And in this failure they break His heart, weaken His church, alienate people from Him and rob themselves of multiplied blessings.

CONCERNING THE SCRIPTURES

Verses 19-21 constitute the second part of Simon Peter's last will and testament for his Christian friends. He speaks about his own convictions concerning the Scripture, especially the prophetic aspects of it. What he has to say revolves around three pivotal words: inspiration, verification and admonition.

Inspiration

In verses 20,21 the Big Fisherman discusses his theory of inspiration of the Scriptures. He states, "But know this first of all, that no prophecy of Scripture is a matter of one's own interpretation, for no proph-

181

ecy was ever made by an act of human will." Barclay wrote, "Many of the early scholars took this to mean when any of the prophets interpreted any situation in history, or when they told how history was going to unfold itself they were not expressing a private opinion of their own; they were passing on to man a revelation which God had given to them."[2]

With this one statement Peter puts the "big lie" to the humanistic theories of inspiration which ascribes the origin of the Bible to the ingenuity of the human mind.

The Bible is not of human origin but of divine origin. Notice the last part of this verse, "but men moved by the Holy Spirit spoke from God." The word "moved" is the present middle participle form of the verb *phero* which basically means "to bring" or "to convey." The significance of this word is seen in the familiar story recorded in Mark 2:1-5. The friends of the paralytic carried him along until they finally placed him at the feet of Jesus. Just so the Holy Spirit carried the scriptural writers along, guiding them, guarding them and providing for them until they completed the manuscripts or letters that He wanted them to write. Peter's theory of inspiration was simply that the Holy Spirit through the human authors produced God's authentic and authoritative message for man, the Bible.

In evangelical circles today three theories of inspiration have been developed which largely have grown out of this one.

The first is the *amanuensis* or dictation theory. According to this the Holy Spirit used human authors as secretaries through whom He dictated the Scriptures. The problem with this theory is that it doesn't account for the difference in styles of writing in the various books. The personality of each of the authors definitely comes through in the books or book he has written.

The second is the verbal plenary theory of inspiration. Simply stated this theory teaches that the authors were directed in their choice of words and that each part of the Bible is equally inspired. For example, the Song of Solomon or the book of Lamentations are just as inspired as the Gospel of John. This theory gives a little more latitude to the human authors in the use of words than does the amanuensis theory, but not much more.

The third is the dynamic theory of inspiration. According to this theory the thoughts and not the words are inspired. The dynamic theorists have to face the question, "How do you convey thoughts apart from words?"

If you were to ask me which of these theories is correct, I would answer, "None," and then tell you this story. One day in a seminary class our theology professor kept talking about the dynamic theory being correct. In doing so he pointed out that it was the thought patterns in the Scripture that conveyed the great spiritual concepts, not the specific words.

At this point I raised my hand and asked the professor, "Would you say the Spirit of God so guarded the words the human authors used that they could not misconvey the thought?" He responded in the affirmative. To me this is the correct theory of inspiration. This is what Peter had in mind when he wrote, ". . . but men moved by the Holy Spirit spoke from God."

Verification

In the first part of verse 19 Peter writes, "And so we have the prophetic word made more sure." Here he is referring again to his experience with the Lord Jesus on the Mount of Transfiguration. It was there he saw in miniature the kingdom which our Lord is going to establish at His second coming. Peter is saying that we can have confidence that the Bible is the authentic Word of God because of fulfilled prophecy.

The prophets spoke of the future with knowledge given to them by God Himself. For example, 700 years before the coming of Christ, Isaiah prophesied His virgin birth (see Isa. 7:14), and 1,000 years before His first advent David pictured His crucifixion (see Psalm 22).

Admonition

Because Peter realizes that the Scripture is reliable and is the authentic Word of God he admonishes his readers to live by its sacred teachings until the Lord returns. He expresses this in the last part of verse 19 where he writes, "to which you do well to pay attention as to a lamp shining in a dark place, until the day dawns and the morning star arises in your hearts."

Peter speaks of the Scripture as being a lamp that shines in a dark place. This place is the society of which you and I are a part. Our society is in darkness and the only light available is the Scripture which points to Jesus Christ as the answer to man's needs. He, the living Word, revealed by the Bible, the written Word, can dispel the darkness in your life.

Thank God for the light that is shining in our dark society. Wise is the person who like the Psalmist says, "Thy word is a lamp to my feet, and a light to my path" (Ps. 119:105).

Footnotes
1. E. H. Bancroft, *Christian Theology* (Grand Rapids: Zondervan Publishing House, 1949), p. 289.
2. Barclay, *The Letters of James and Peter*, p. 368.

12

---

2 Peter 2:1-22

THE EIGHT CHARACTERISTICS
OF FALSE TEACHERS

In this chapter Peter calls to our attention four significant truths related to false teachers—he points out eight characteristics of false teachers; he assures us that the Lord is able to deliver the righteous from the temptations put before them by false teachers; he issues a warning to those who are tempted to follow false teachers; he guarantees the ultimate destruction of those who are false teachers.

"But false prophets also arose among the people, just as there will also be false teachers among you, who will secretly introduce destructive heresies, even denying the Master who bought them, bringing swift destruction upon themselves. And many will follow their sensuality, and because of them the way of the truth will be maligned; and in their greed they will exploit you with false words; their judgment from

long ago is not idle, and their destruction is not asleep
. . . and especially those who indulge the flesh in
its corrupt desires and despise authority. Daring,
self-willed, they do not tremble when they revile
angelic majesties, whereas angels who are greater in
might and power do not bring a reviling judgment
against them before the Lord. But these, like unreasoning animals, born as creatures of instinct to be
captured and killed, reviling where they have no
knowledge, will in the destruction of those creatures
also be destroyed, suffering wrong as the wages of
doing wrong. They count it a pleasure to revel in
the daytime. They are stains and blemishes, reveling
in their deceptions, as they carouse with you; having
eyes full of adultery and that never cease from sin;
enticing unstable souls, having a heart trained in
greed, accursed children; forsaking the right way they
have gone astray, having followed the way of Balaam,
the son of Beor, who loved the wages of unrighteousness, but he received a rebuke for his own trans-
gression; for a dumb donkey, speaking with a voice
of a man, restrained the madness of the prophet.
These are springs without water, and mists driven
by a storm, for whom the black darkness has been
reserved. For speaking out arrogant words of vanity
they entice by fleshly desires, by sensuality, those who
barely escape from the ones who live in error, promis-
ing them freedom while they themselves are slaves
of corruption; for by what a man is overcome, by
this he is enslaved" (vv. 1-3,10-19).

As we begin our consideration of the subject of
false teachers, the question will arise, "How can I
distinguish the false from the true?" And the answer

is, "By knowing the eight characteristics of the false."
Not all eight characteristics apply to all false teachers,
but all eight of these characteristics can be found
in the various false teachers who seek to sell their
wares to Christians. What are they?

Subtle 1.

A false teacher is very subtle in the way he ap-
proaches his victim. He doesn't come right out and
say, "What you believe is wrong!" No, he is much
smoother and much more clever than that. Peter
describes him in verse 1. Notice especially the phrase,
"will secretly introduce." It is the translation of the
Greek word, *pareisazousin,* which means "to introduce
stealthily," or "to introduce subtly." This verb is in
the future tense indicating continuous action.

Notice also the word, "heresies"; it comes from
the Greek noun, *hairesis,* which means "choices." He
modifies this with the adjective, "destructive," speaking of destructive choices. In using these two Greek
words together in effect Peter is saying, "The false
teachers very subtly using a softsell will keep gentle
pressure on you seeking to get you to buy their
destructive choices instead of God's sound teaching."
They follow the softsell, subtle-pitch example Satan
set for them when he deceived Eve in the Garden
of Eden. (See Gen. 3:1.)

Sensual 2.

In the second place Simon Peter points out that
false teachers are characterized by sensuality. Not all
false teachers are sensual but there are many who
are. The word translated "sensuality" in verse two

is *aselgeiais.* Thayer translates the word, "unbridled lust," "licentiousness," "lasciviousness," "wantonness." The word definitely describes those of low moral standards.

Peter tells us in this verse that the Christians who succumb to the sensuality taught by false teachers do irreparable damage to the cause of Christ. He says in essence, "Because of the Christians who practice the sensuality of false teachers, Jesus Christ is maligned." This last word is a translation of the verb *blasphemeo* from which we get our English word "blasphemed."

In verse 10 Peter speaks of these sensual false teachers as those who indulge the flesh in its corrupt desires. The phrase "in its corrupt desires" is a translation of *epithumia miasmou,* which means "in the lust of pollution." There are some false teachers who indulge the flesh in the lust of pollution. I can think of no better word to describe either perverted sex or sex out of wedlock. In God's sight normal sex within marriage is beautiful, wholesome, clean and pure; but sex out of wedlock, or perverted sex is something else. It is pollution.

Peter describes the sensual false teachers as "having eyes full of adultery," or literally, "They have eyes which are full of an adulteress." This means that they see in every woman the possibility of being an adulteress.

We have this kind of false teacher today. The most obvious examples are those who are devil worshipers. Illicit sex, sometimes called free sex, plays a large role in what they do. Let me quote Anton LaVey, "Since worship of fleshly things produces pleasure,

there would then be a temple of glorious indul-
gence. . . ."[1]

In addition to Anton LaVey there are other false
teachers selling sensuality, those who subscribe to the
philosophy known as "Situation Ethics" or "The New
Morality."

Basic morality is ebbing away in our nation and
the only thing that is going to stop this tide is for
Christians to take a firm stand against it. This we
must do by the quality of lives we live and the message we speak.

Greedy 3.

Greed is the third characteristic of false teachers
which Simon Peter calls to our attention in verse 3.
Pleonexia, the Greek word, comes from two words,
pleon—"mine" and *exo*—"to have." Thayer in trans-
lating the word says that it actually means "one eager
to have more, especially of that which belongs to
others."[2] It can also be translated "covetousness."

Emporeusontai, the word "exploit," means "to deceive for one's own advantage." The verb is in the
future tense indicating a continuous action. It can
be translated, "They constantly deceive for their own
advantage." *Plastois logois* is the phrase translated
"with false words." It can also be translated, "with
well-turned words."

In putting all of this together we discover that
Simon Peter is saying, "And being exceedingly cove-
tous, these false teachers, being slick-tongue artists
deceive the general public with well-turned words in
order that they might become rich." The same idea
is found in the last part of verse 14. Because their

hearts are trained in greed they entice others to follow them and as the result they become accursed children in God's eyes.

Peter cites an example from the Old Testament in verses 15 and 16 of this type of false teacher. This reference takes us back into the book of Numbers, chapters 22-31, to the story of Balaam.

In the story three things are apparent. First, even though Balaam never cursed Israel, he had a strong desire to do so because of the personal gain he would derive from it. Second, when he had the opportunity, he persuaded the people of Israel to worship Baal, and her men to become involved with the women of Moab; God greatly punished Israel because of this. And third, there is a strong inference in the story that Balaam received a handsome reward for doing this. He was a slick-tongue artist who for personal gain sold the people of Israel a bill of goods.

Despises Authority 4.

Peter informs us that false teachers despise authority. The word translated "to despise" comes from the Greek verb *kataphroneo* which means "to despise in the sense of disregarding."

In Peter's day there were teachers who claimed that the grace of God was inexhaustible and limitless, and Christians could live as they pleased. They were no longer under law but under grace. They had the right to disregard completely those sections in God's Word which place limitations on their life-style. They overlooked the teaching of Jesus that He had not come to destroy the law but to fulfill it.

It didn't seem to enter their minds that one day

every Christian will stand before the judgment seat of Christ and give an account of all of his activities and every idle word that he has spoken. They lived and taught that a Christian had the right to do anything he desired. They disregarded the authority of the Scripture which teaches that the Christian is to be careful about his influence, always making sure that it counts for the Saviour.

Self-willed

In verse 10 Peter tells us that false teachers are self-willed. This is a translation of the noun *authades* which comes from two words, *autos* meaning "self" and *hedone* meaning "pleasing." The false teachers are self-pleasers. They don't care about either God or man. Their number one and only concern is for themselves. They will lie, steal and cheat. They will do anything to get what they want. They will even preach the gospel, although they don't live by it, in order to feather their own nest.

Daring

The sixth characteristic of false teachers is that they are daring. Notice how Peter puts this in verse 10. The word "to revile" is a translation of *blasphemeo*, from which the English word blaspheme is derived. A good synonym for daring is brazen.

In verse 11 Peter contrasts the attitude and activity of false teachers with that of angels who are greater in might and power than they. He probably is referring to Jude 9. There we read, "But Michael the archangel, when he disputed with the devil and argued about the body of Moses did not dare pronounce

195

against him a railing judgment, but said, 'The Lord rebuke you.' "

William Barclay in commenting on this has written, "The point is that even an angel so great as Michael would not bring an evil charge against an angel so dark as Satan. He left the matter to God. If Michael did not despise and slander an evil angel, how can man bring slanderous charges against the angels of God?"[3]

Meaningless 7.

The message of false teachers is meaningless. It has no substance; it is not based on fact. In the first part of verse 18 Peter refers to them as "speaking out arrogant words of vanity." This is the reason that he refers to them in verse 17 as "springs without water, and mists driven by a storm." Of what value is a spring without water or a heavy mist driven away by a storm? The answer obviously is none. And so it is with the message of a false teacher; it is of no value whatsoever.

Dishonest 8.

Last but not least Peter informs us that false teachers are dishonest. He states this in a most unusual and meaningful way. In effect Peter is saying here, "False teachers promise real freedom, but they can't deliver for they themselves are not free. They are slaves to corruption." A false teacher cannot give true freedom because he doesn't have it.

The opposite of this is also true. A person can give that which he does have—true freedom from superstition, from the penalty of sin, and from the fear of the future. It is available through Jesus Christ.

DELIVERANCE FROM FALSE TEACHERS

Peter makes it quite plain that the Lord is able to deliver the Christian from the temptations and testings with which he is confronted by false teachers. This he does very graphically through the use of two Old Testament illustrations.

The first centers in Noah. In verse 5 and in the first part of verse 9 we read, "and did not spare the ancient world, but preserved Noah, a preacher of righteousness, with seven others, when He brought a flood upon the world of the ungodly . . . then the Lord knows how to rescue the godly from temptation."

There are two words here that we need to consider. The first is "preserved." Peter tells us that God preserved Noah and seven others, his wife and his three sons and their wives, during the time He completely inundated the world. This actually comes from the Greek verb *Phulasso* which means "to keep safe."

The second word is "rescue." Peter informs us that the Lord knows how to rescue the godly from temptation. This word comes from the Greek verb *ruomai* which literally means "to drag us out of danger." In the Sermon on the Mount Jesus taught His disciples to pray, "And do not lead us into temptation, but deliver us from evil" or drag us out of danger.

When we put this all together, Simon Peter was saying, "Take a look at Noah. He was a preacher of righteousness who, while building the ark faithfully, proclaimed to the people that judgment was coming. When that moment came that the Almighty opened up the fountains of the deep and poured down the rain from above Noah had nothing to fear. Even though every other man, woman and child perished in the flood, God saw to it that Noah and his family were kept in safety. Now just as the Almighty did this for Noah's family, just so He is able to drag the Christians, the godly, out of the dangers to which false teachers subject them."

The second illustration focuses our attention on Lot (see verses 6-9). The people in Sodom and Gomorrah are described here as being "unprincipled." This word is a translation of *Ton athesmon en aselgeia* which means "of the lawless in outrageous behavior." Peter is making the point that the people who lived in the twin cities were seeking to contaminate Lot and everyone else with whom they came in contact by their immoral, unethical, lawless, unprincipled conduct.

This was the type of thing Lot faced. Ultimately it brought God's judgment upon the cities. But just before it happened God rescued Lot. Here again we meet the word, *ruomai*. He literally dragged Lot out of those cities before they were destroyed.

In verse 9 Peter points out that the same God who dragged Lot out of those burning cities is able to deliver the Christian from the fires of temptation and testing with which false teachings surround him.

WARNING TO FOLLOWERS
OF FALSE TEACHERS

The Big Fisherman issues a strong warning to any who is tempted to follow the teaching of those who are antithetical to Christ. "For if after they have escaped the defilements of the world by the knowledge of the Lord and Saviour Jesus Christ, they are again entangled in them and are overcome, the last state has become worse for them than the first. For it would be better for them not to have known the way of righteousness, than having known it, to turn away from the holy commandment delivered to them. It has happened to them according to the true proverb, 'A dog returns to its own vomit,' and, 'A sow, after washing, returns to wallowing in the mire' " (vv. 20-22).

We need to be very careful in understanding that Peter is not talking here about people who have been saved and then have lost their salvation because they have turned their backs upon Christ. In the first part of verse 20 we have an unfortunate translation. In the original there is no definite article with the word "knowledge" and the preposition "by" is not used. Instead it is the preposition "in." In the interest of accuracy this part of verse 20 should be translated, "For if after they escaped the defilements of the world in knowledge of the Lord and Saviour Jesus Christ." In other words what Peter is driving at here is this: there are many who, because they have a general knowledge of the teachings of our Lord Jesus Christ and what He can do for them, actually at times live on a high moral and ethical plain. They haven't experienced regeneration, only reformation. They live a very decent life for a while, but ultimately they return to their old ways. They have no spiritual power within them to cause them to do otherwise.

Concerning these he tells us two things: first, when they turn and follow false teachers their last state

199

becomes worse than their first; and second, it would have been better for these people if they had never known anything about Jesus Christ at all.

Luke 12:48 provides the reason for this. There Jesus states, "And from everyone who has been given much shall much be required; and to whom they entrusted much, of him they will ask all the more." Although this is usually applied to Christian stewardship, it is also applicable to salvation. The individual who has had the greatest opportunity to commit his life to Christ and has chosen instead to follow a false teacher will receive the greatest punishment.

Peter points out in chapter 2 that false teachers will ultimately come under the punitive judgment of almighty God. "Their judgment from long ago is not idle, and their destruction is not asleep." *The Living Bible* paraphrase makes the meaning of this clear, "But God condemned them long ago and their destruction is on the way" (v. 3).

In verses 4-6 Peter gives three illustrations in the form of conditional clauses of what God is going to do to them, and he concludes each of these conditional clauses in the last part of verse 9. "For if God did not spare angels when they sinned, but cast them into hell and committed them to pits of darkness, reserved for judgment . . . then the Lord knows how to . . . keep the unrighteous under punishment for the day of judgment."

Peter tells us that when the angels sinned God did not spare them but cast them into hell and committed them to pits of darkness reserved for judgment. The usual word for "hell" in the New Testament is either *Hades* or *Gehenna;* but this is not the word Peter uses here. He used *tartarus* which in Greek mythology refers to the lowest and most terrible hell. In the biblical context it pictures that part of hell in which the severest punishment is administered.

The word translated "pits" is the Greek word *siros* which means a pit in which a wild animal is trapped. Peter is saying, "Since God had the power to throw the rebellious angels into that part of hell which is like a pit of darkness in which wild animals are trapped, keeping them there until the time of judgment, then you can be assured that He is able to keep all false teachers under punishment for the day of judgment."

In verse 5 Peter uses the illustration of the flood. In combining this verse with 9 he is actually saying, "If God was able to judge the world with a flood, destroying all but eight people, then surely He has the ability to keep all false teachers under punishment for the day of judgment."

In verse 6 he uses the example of Sodom and Gomorrah. Putting verses 6 and 9 together we discover that Peter is emphasizing the fact that just as God had the power to judge Sodom and Gomorrah, reducing them to ashes, He has the power to keep all false teachers under punishment until the day of judgment.

The question naturally arises, "What did Peter mean specifically when he said that God knows how to keep the unrighteous under punishment for the day of judgment?" The Bible clearly answers this. A false teacher when he dies goes immediately to hades where he suffers the same punishment that the rich man experienced after his death. Jesus described this for us in Luke 16:19-31.

This punishment continues until after the satanic rebellion is put down following the millennium. At that time all the unsaved will be raised to face Jesus at the Great White Throne judgment which is described in Revelation 20:11-15. The purpose of this judgment is to assign the degrees of punishment which each one will receive throughout all of eternity. This will be the most severe judgment any man will ever experience and the sentences will be eternal.

Now just in case you and I miss the point of this Peter states it in a slightly different way, "But these, like unreasoning animals, born as creatures of instinct to be captured and killed, reviling where they have no knowledge, will in the destruction of those creatures also be destroyed" (v. 12). A more accurate translation of the last part of this verse is, "will in their corruption be corrupted." They will be corrupted not in the sense they will cease to exist but in the sense of going into a worse state. Peter emphasizes the fact that eternally false teachers will experience the most severe punishment imaginable in hell.

Throughout this second chapter Peter constantly implies that there are two types of teachers making their appeal to men: the false and the true, the godless and the godly, the dishonest and the honest, the anti-biblical and the biblical. Those who choose to follow the false will suffer the fate of the false. Those who choose to follow the true will share in the pleasures and joys of the true. Wise is the person who chooses this second alternative, for his eternal destiny is secure in Christ Jesus.

202

Footnotes

1. LaVey, Anton Sandor, *The Satanic Bible.*
2. Thayer, *Greek English Lexicon of the New Testament,* p. 516.
3. Barclay, *The Letters of James and Peter,* p. 383.

13

2 Peter 3:1-18

THE FUTURE OF OUR WORLD

The late President Dwight D. Eisenhower once made the statement, "I am interested in the future because that is where I am going to spend the remainder of my life." Simon Peter was also interested in the future. In the third chapter of his second epistle he speaks about it in a forthright manner. He points out that our present world is going to be destroyed by fire and will be replaced by new heavens and a new earth in which righteousness dwells.

The Earth's Destruction

The language which he uses in describing the earth's destruction is most graphic. "But the present heavens and earth by His word are being reserved for fire, kept for the day of judgment and destruction of ungodly men" (v. 7). The identity of the one referred to as His Word is none other than our Lord Jesus Christ Himself. According to John it was He who brought the heavens and earth into existence (see John 1:1-3). Peter says it is He who will keep them until that moment when they shall be consumed with fire, and the enemies of righteousness destroyed. He expresses it this way, "But the day of the Lord will come like a thief, in which the heavens will pass away with a roar and the elements will be destroyed with intense heat, and the earth and its works will be burned up" (v. 10).

Peter points out three important considerations. It is impossible to pinpoint the time when this destruction of the heavens and the earth by fire will take place. It will come upon man like a thief. It will come upon him when he is neither looking for it nor expecting it.

The destruction will be accompanied by a loud roar. The word translated "roar" is from the Greek *roizedon* which means "a crackling roar," like the crackling sound of a forest on fire. The elements of the heavens and the earth will be destroyed with intense heat to the point of actually being burned up.

Peter describes the destruction as he writes, "looking for and hastening the coming of the day of God, on account of which the heavens will be destroyed by burning, and the elements will melt with intense heat" (v. 12). The verb "to melt" is from the Greek *teko* which means "to render liquid." In liquid form creation as we know it will be no more.

Prior to Hiroshima men of science laughed at the thought of the heavens and earth being destroyed.

But no more! The temperature of the sun is 36,000,000° F while the interior temperature of an H-bomb is 90,000,000° F.

The Christian's Preparation

The major thrust of this third chapter of Second Peter is the truth that the present heavens and earth are rushing pell mell toward their destruction by fire and their replacement with new heavens and a new earth. Simon Peter calls to our attention seven very practical considerations: (1) A major duty of every pastor, Sunday School teacher and spiritual leader (vv. 1,2); (2) The type of mind every Christian should have (v. 1); (3) The attitude of skeptics as they are confronted with the truth of our Lord's second coming (vv. 3,4); (4) The inconsistency of this attitude (vv. 5-7); (5) God's evaluation of time (v. 8); (6) Two outstanding characteristics of our Lord (v. 9); (7) Advice to Christians in the light of that which is coming in the future.

First, the Big Fisherman calls to our attention a major duty of every pastor, Sunday School teacher, and spiritual leader. "This now, beloved, the second letter I am writing to you in which I am stirring up your sincere mind by way of reminder, that you should remember the words spoken beforehand by the holy prophets and the commandment of the Lord and Saviour spoken by your apostles" (vv. 1,2).

The verb "to stir up" is a translation of *diegeiro* which means "to arouse, to awake thoroughly." In using this word, Peter in effect was saying, "As your spiritual leader I am going to make sure that you are kept awake mentally both as to what the prophets taught in the Old Testament and what Jesus commanded as this information has been relayed to you by His apostles. This I am going to do by constantly reviewing this material with you. I am going to go over it and over it and over it again so that you will have no difficulty in remembering it."

In the second place, Peter points out the type of mind every Christian should have. "This is now, beloved, the second letter I am writing to you in which I am stirring up your sincere mind by way of reminder." The Christian is to have a "sincere" mind. The Greek for this is *eilikrine,* and it means "that which is being viewed in the sunshine and is found clear and pure."

"Sincere" also has a Latin source, *sine*—"without" and *cere*—"wax." In the days of the great Roman sculptors there were unscrupulous men who did not bother to fix a nick, they simply filled it in with wax. Some artisans were above this. If they made a mistake on a piece of marble, they spent days working it out with chisel and hammer. These men were known as "sincere" sculptors, or "sculptors without wax." Their work could be subjected to the brightest sunlight and found to be pure.

The Christian's mind is to be clean and pure. Paul commanded, "Let this mind be in you, which was also in Christ Jesus"† (Phil. 2:5). When Jesus was asked what the great commandment in the law was, He responded, "Thou shalt love the Lord thy God with all thy heart, and with all thy soul, and with all thy mind"† (Matt. 22:37). This is impossible unless the mind is free of evil thoughts.

Paul informs us as to how we as Christians can

have sincere, pure minds. He writes, "Finally, brethren, whatever is true, whatever is honorable, whatever is right, whatever is pure, whatever is lovely, whatever is of good repute, if there is any excellence and if anything worthy of praise, let your mind dwell on these things" (Phil. 4:8).

The mind is like a glass. If there is any dirty water in the glass, the best way to clean it is to rinse it out continually by running pure water through it. If this process is continued long enough, the filthy water is removed and replaced with clean, pure, water. David portrays a happy man, "But his delight is in the law of the Lord, and in His law he meditates day and night" (Psalm 1:2). Usually I listen to one of the news stations or old-time, popular favorites on my car radio. I decided this time could be better used by listening to Scripture on a tape recorder. I am literally filling my mind with thoughts that are true, honorable, right, pure, lovely and of good report. In so doing I find there is no room for any other type of thinking. And there is one more thing I want to say. This cleansing of the mind process can only begin after you have surrendered your heart and mind to Jesus Christ.

Paul wrote, "Therefore if any man is in Christ, he is a new creature; the old things passed away; behold, new things have come" (2 Cor. 5:17). One of the things that passes away is the desire to fill your mind with filth. Instead you long to have the mind of Christ, to think thoughts after Him.

Third, Peter points out the usual attitude taken by skeptics when they are confronted with the truth of our Lord's second coming. "Know this first of all,

211

that in the last days mockers will come with their mocking, following after their own lusts, and saying, 'Where is the promise of His coming? For ever since the fathers fell asleep, all continues just as it was from the beginning' " (vv. 3,4).

The word translated "mockers" comes from the Greek *empaiktai* which means "a mocker, a derider, a scoffer, a skeptic." The verbal form of this word is *empaizo* which literally means "to play with, to trifle with."

Peter tells us that one of the signs of the last days will be scoffers, skeptics trifling with the idea of the second coming of Christ, playing with the concept of our Lord's return to the point of laughing at it. He calls to our attention both the reason for the skeptics taking this attitude and the argument they use against our Lord's second coming.

The reason is found in the last part of verse 3: "following after their own lusts." They are so busy with their own fleshly desires, they will neither have the time nor the inclination to consider seriously any spiritual truth. They could care less that someday they are going to answer to God for their actions. Life right now for them is a bowl of cherries, and they are eating it to the full.

When people like this are confronted with the fact of our Lord's return, they trifle with it. They play with it. They argue against it by saying, "Where is the promise of His coming? For ever since the fathers fell asleep, all continues just as it was from the beginning of creation." They laugh at the idea that the Lord might come again. They say, the first man married and produced children, and died. His chil-

212

dren married and produced children and died. And so the cycles have continued throughout history without any cataclysmic interruption, and will continue in the same way. It is ludicrous to think that anything else is possible.

This brings us to our fourth practical consideration. In verses 5 and 6 Peter points out the inconsistency of this attitude and argument. He writes, "For when they maintain this, it escapes their notice that by the word of God the heavens existed long ago and the earth was formed out of water and by water, through which the world at that time was destroyed, being flooded with water."

Peter calls two facts to our attention. First, the Word of God, who is none other than the Lord Jesus Christ, formed the earth out of water. According to Genesis 1:9 He actually drew it out of water. Second, the argument of the skeptics that there never has been a cataclysmic interruption of history is nonsense, for the world at one time was destroyed by water. Peter refers specifically to the flood described in Genesis 6—9. In the latter part of chapter 7 Moses makes it clear that every part of the earth was involved. In verse 19 he writes, "And the water prevailed more and more upon the earth, so that all the high mountains everywhere under the heavens were covered." Again in verses 23,24 the universality of the flood is underscored. "Thus He blotted out every living thing that was upon the face of the land. . . . And the water prevailed upon the earth one hundred and fifty days."

In the fifth place, Peter gives us an insight into God's evaluation of time. "But do not let this one fact escape your notice, beloved, that with the Lord one day is as a thousand years, and a thousand years as one day" (v. 8). This is but a New Testament statement of the truth spelled out in Psalm 90:4.

Do you see the picture which verse 8 suggests? In verses 3 and 4 Simon Peter points out that in the last days there will be skeptics who will laugh at the idea of the second coming of Christ. After answering them, Peter speaks to some of his exiled Christian brothers and sisters who may be troubled by the delay in the Lord's return. Rather than being skeptical about it, perhaps they were despondent. Thirty years have passed since His ascension and nothing has happened.

In responding Peter calls them, "Beloved." I like that. It comes from the Greek *agapetoi* and is used in Matthew 3:16,17 by God the Father in referring to our Lord Jesus Christ. The verbal form of this word is *agapao,* meaning "to love in the highest sense." It is the verb used in John 3:16. In addressing his persecuted Christian friends as "Beloved," in effect Peter was saying, "You my brothers and sisters in Christ whom I love with a godly passion (and this is the way each and every Christian should love his fellow Christians): Don't overlook the fact that our Lord doesn't measure time as you and I do. One day with Him is as a thousand years and a thousand years as one day. He has not chosen to reveal the time of His coming. He has simply stated that He will return and that believers should be watching for Him."

The whole point of verse 8 is to assure the Christians of Peter's day and the Christians of our day that God is not in a hurry. Despite the criticism of skeptics and what may appear to be a delay, God's prophetic program is moving ahead and will continue to do so until the present heavens and earth are destroyed and replaced with new heavens and a new earth. And pivotal to this prophetic plan is the second coming of Jesus Christ.

While it is true that the Almighty has not chosen to reveal the time of the Saviour's return He has outlined signs of His coming. Studying these signs is one of the most exciting and at the same time spiritually rewarding studies that the believer can make.

Our Lord rebuked the religious leaders of His day for their inability to interpret the signs of His Messiahship at His first coming. "And the Pharisees and the Sadducees came up, and testing Him asked Him to show them a sign from heaven. But He answered and said to them, 'When it is evening, you say, "It will be fair weather, for the sky is red." And in the morning, "There will be a storm today, for the sky is red and threatening." Do you know how to discern the appearance of the sky, but cannot discern the signs of the times?' " (Matt. 16:1-3).

Just as Christ expected His contemporaries in Judaism to discern the signs of His Messiahship, just so He expects Christians to discern the signs of His return.

One of the most competent scholars in this field in our day is Hal Lindsey. In his book, *The Late Great Planet Earth,* Hal tells of a conversation with an Air Force colonel. The Colonel said that three weeks before, someone had shoved a copy of *The*

Late Great Planet Earth into his hands. And he said, "I didn't intend to read it, because frankly I am irreligious. I started reading it, and found I couldn't put it down. It scared the hell out of me."

Hal said, "I hope I can take you literally."

He said, "I'm in the Pentagon, in the war room, Air Force intelligence. I have to stay abreast of the latest top-secret information. I knew you didn't have access to this information, and yet you set forth a pattern that is exactly what we see coming. When I got to the end I did something else you talked about. I got on my knees and accepted Jesus Christ."

Yes, the Lord is coming, and wise is the person that does exactly what that colonel did.

In the sixth place Peter speaks of two outstanding characteristics of our Lord: First, He is patient, and second, He is redemptive. "The Lord is not slow about His promise, as some count slowness, but is patient toward you, not wishing for any to perish but for all to come to repentance" (2 Peter 3:9). Peter is saying here, "Don't think that the reason our Lord has not yet returned is because He is slow in keeping His promises. You need to be aware that He is patient toward you and every other person. His great desire is to give every man, woman and child as much time as possible in which to repent of sin and receive by faith the gift of eternal redemption which He purchased for them on Calvary."

This clear teaching pulls the rug out from under the idea that God has elected some to be saved and others to be lost. Look closely at the last part of verse 9. In referring to Jesus, Peter writes, ". . . not wishing for any to perish but for all to come to repentance."

The meaning here is clear. If a person eternally perishes it is not because Christ wills it, but because he wills it.

The teaching of 2 Peter 3:9 is that God is delaying our Lord's coming in order to give people who have thus far rejected Him more time in which to rectify this situation. Of a woman by the name of Jezebel who was a false teacher, our Lord says, "And I gave her time to repent" (Rev. 2:21). If you are not a Christian, this is exactly what the Lord is doing for you at the present. The main reason He is letting you breathe is to give you an opportunity to get right with Him. God help you to take advantage of it now. Don't delay. You can never know what a day will bring forth.

In the seventh place, Simon Peter offers some good advice to Christians in the light of what is coming in the future. "Since all these things are to be destroyed in this way, what sort of people ought you to be in holy conduct and godliness, looking for and hastening the coming of the day of God, on account of which the heavens will be destroyed by burning, and the elements will melt with intense heat" (2 Pet. 3:11,12).

PETER'S FINAL ADVICE

The first part of this question is, "Since all of these things are to be destroyed in this way, what sort of people ought you to be?" Or to put this personally, "Since we know that the present heavens and earth are to be destroyed by fire and replaced by new heavens and a new earth wherein dwells righteousness, what type of Christians should you and I

217

be?" Peter devotes the remaining part of verses 11 and 12 and verses 14-18 to answering this question. In so doing he points out that the Christian life is to be marked in five ways: (1) By personal holiness; (2) By inner peace; (3) By evangelistic zeal; (4) By doctrinal steadfastness; (5) By growth in grace and knowledge.

(1) The Christian's life is to be marked by *personal holiness*. Peter speaks to this point in verse 11 where he uses both the phrase "in holy conduct" and the word "godliness" to describe it. In verse 14, he also tells us that the believer is to be spotless or pure and blameless or irreprehensible. Yes, his life is to be marked by holy living. *Hagios* is the word used for "holy" in the New Testament. It actually means "to be separate from common conduct and use." A Christian is one who is unwilling to live by the base standards of ethics and morals accepted by the majority. He separates himself from these in that he lives above them. His directives for the conduct of his life are found in such great biblical passages as the Ten Commandments and the Sermon on the Mount.

Peter makes a suggestion in verse 12 aimed at helping the Christian in this regard. "Looking for" is a translation of *prosdokontas* which means "to look in the sense that you really expect it to happen." The believer who is constantly looking for our Lord's return and ultimately the new heavens and the new earth will discover that this has a purifying effect upon his life. The apostle John writes, "We know that, if He should appear, we shall be like Him, because we shall see Him just as He is. And every one who has this hope fixed on Him purifies himself, just as He is pure" (1 John 3:2,3).

Just as the POW's families knocked themselves out to do what they knew would make their loved ones happy when they returned, just so the Christian who daily looks for and expects the Lord's second coming will prepare for it by doing what he knows will please Him. You can rest assured that he will not be engaging in questionable activities. His life will be one of personal holiness.

The Christian's life is to be marked by *peace.* "Therefore, beloved, since you look for these things, be diligent to be found by Him in peace" (v. 14). Following His resurrection Jesus appeared to His disciples in the upper room and greeted them with the words, "Peace be with you" (John 20:21). Prior to His crucifixion He said to them, "Peace I leave with you; My peace I give you; not as the world gives, do I give to you. Let not your heart be troubled; nor let it be fearful" (John 14:27). The Christian who allows the Holy Spirit to guide him in his daily walk has godly peace within, regardless of what the circumstances on the outside may be. This he does because the Spirit of God keeps him in constant contact with the Saviour, who is the source of peace.

Evangelistic zeal is the third mark of the Christian who is truly getting ready for our Lord's coming. Simon Peter spells this out in the first part of verse 15, "And regard the patience of our Lord to be salvation." *The Living Bible*'s paraphrase makes this clear, "And remember why he is waiting. He is giving us time to get his message of salvation out to others."

During the post-Resurrection ministry of our Lord,

His disciples came to Him and asked when He was going to establish His kingdom. After telling them that this was entirely in the hands of the Father who had not chosen to reveal it, He said, "But you shall receive power when the Holy Spirit has come upon you; and you shall be My witnesses both in Jerusalem, and in all Judea and Samaria, and even to the remotest part of the earth" (Acts 1:8). It is interesting to note that this is not a command. The verb is not in the imperative mood but in the indicative. It is a statement of fact. In it in effect Jesus is saying, "When you are really filled with the Holy Spirit, the perfectly normal and natural thing for you to do is to share your faith with others whether you be in Jerusalem, Judea, Samaria, or any other place in the world."

(4) In the fourth place the Christian's life is to be marked by *doctrinal steadfastness*. "Just as also our beloved brother Paul, according to the wisdom given him, wrote to you, as also in all his letters, speaking in them of these things, in which are some things hard to understand, which the untaught and unstable distort, as they do also the rest of the Scriptures, to their own destruction. You therefore, beloved, knowing this beforehand, be on your guard lest, being carried away by the error of unprincipled men, you fall from your own steadfastness" (vv. 15-17).

Here again the paraphrase of *The Living Bible* is of a great assistance in making clear Peter's teaching, "Our wise and beloved brother Paul has talked about these same things in many of his letters. Some of his comments are not easy to understand, and there are people who are deliberately stupid, and always

220

demand some unusual interpretation—they have twisted his letters around to mean something quite different from what he meant, just as they do the other parts of the Scripture—and the result is disaster for them. I am warning you ahead of time, dear brothers, so that you can watch out and not be carried away by the mistakes of these wicked men, lest you yourselves become mixed up too."

There are some things here we don't want to miss. *
There are people who have maliciously misinterpreted the teachings of Paul. Instead of allowing the text to mean what it says, they have twisted it, and as a result they have brought disaster upon themselves.

Many examples of this readily come to mind. Let me give you just one. Because of Paul's heavy emphasis upon the doctrine of salvation by grace, there have been those who teach that once a person has been saved by grace through faith he can live as he pleases. Many of these people are fundamentalist in doctrine but complete libertines in life-style. They completely overlook Romans 6:1,2 and they forget about Philippians 2:12,13. The probability is that they have never been saved, for Jesus said, "You will know them by their fruits" (Matt. 7:20). Peter tells us in verse 16 that people like this bring about their own destruction.

You and I as Christians are to be forewarned that God expects us to maintain steadfastly a position of doctrinal purity. We are not to be constantly changing our minds about the fundamental truths of the Bible. Like Martin Luther of old our philosophy concerning the teaching of Scripture must be, "Here I stand! I can do no other." This means that we will have thoroughly accepted such truths as the coexistence of

221

Christ with the Father, the virgin birth of our Saviour, His sinless life, His substitutionary death on Calvary, His bodily resurrection, His second coming, salvation by grace and grace alone manifested through righteous living, the inspiration of the Scripture, and the final and eternal reunion of all believers with the Saviour and one another.

(5) In the fifth place, as the Christian looks forward to the new heavens and the new earth he is to mature in the faith. His life is to be marked by a growth in grace and knowledge. Peter makes this clear as he writes in verse 18, "But grow in the grace and in knowledge of our Lord and Saviour Jesus Christ."

To grow in grace means that you and I as Christians will day by day have a growing awareness of our complete dependence upon God's constantly bestowing His favor upon us. The very meaning of grace is unmerited favor. It is God thinking in terms of what we need rather than what we deserve. This growth comes in a daily study of the Scripture whereby we learn the truths which God has revealed to man, a daily involvement in serving Jesus Christ whereby we learn by experience that the principles of the Bible really work.

Here is an article that is germane to this growth in grace and knowledge process. The author points out the differences between a believer and a disciple.

1. To believe is cheap and costs us nothing. But to follow Christ is costly and He asks us to consider the great cost.

2. Believers consider themselves first, but disciples consider Christ first.

222

3. Believers produce no perfect fruit, but disciples are known by their fruit.

4. Belief saves my soul, but discipleship glorifies Christ.

5. Believers are not necessarily known as Christians, but disciples are.

6. Believers go to heaven, but disciples are greatly rewarded there.

7. And to this list I would add one more statement. Believers have not grown in grace and in the knowledge of our Lord and Saviour Jesus Christ, they are spiritual pygmies. Disciples are constantly experiencing a growth in grace and knowledge whereby they are daily maturing in the faith. Notice the way Peter brings this epistle to a close, "To Him be the glory, both now and to the day of eternity. Amen." It is as if he is saying, "My great desire is to have all that I am and all that I do bring glory to my Saviour now and to the day of eternity. Amen."

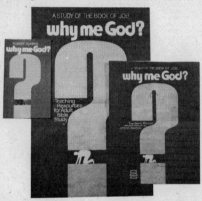

Folk Psalms of Faith

Ray C. Stedman

13 session expository study of 20 Psalms
focuses on the struggles and joys of
God's people. Bible learning activities
relate these "folk songs of faith" to life
today.

Study resources include a teaching manual with
teaching plans and background information; discussion starters and numerous learning activities.

COMPLETE RESOURCE KIT